Collins Phrase Books

FRENCH
GERMAN
ITALIAN
PORTUGUESE
SPANISH
SCANDINAVIAN
RUSSIAN
GREEK
YUGOSLAV
DUTCH

COLLINS PHRASE BOOKS

FRENCH

Compiled by

Edwin Carpenter
with
Philippe Patry

COLLINS
LONDON & GLASGOW

First Published 1981
Fifth Reprint 1984

Cover photographs
by courtesy of
Van Phillips
and J. Allan Cash Ltd.

ISBN 0 00 433968 1
© William Collins Sons & Co. Ltd. 1981
Printed in Great Britain
Collins Clear-Type Press

Contents

Contents

Introduction

For this Phrase Book, we hope we've thought of *almost* everything. If you can't speak French, the Collins French Phrase Book can help you say what you want whenever you want.

We've thought of what you'll be doing – driving and parking the car, having a drink in a café, buying stamps for your postcards. Each page has a clear heading so you can find your place quickly, and each section contains the phrases you are genuinely likely to need.

We've put ourselves in your shoes and tried to think of the situations that could catch you out. Have you ever been faced with an exotic dish and wanted to know the right way to eat it? or how to ask for a babysitter? These are just the kind of practical questions that you'll find here. And they are in simple but idiomatic French, with an easy-to-read pronunciation included.

Besides questions and phrases, we give you the information you need. Many sections begin with a few helpful tips on subjects like using the telephone or travelling by bus. There's a guide to food and wine, so you'll know what to try out, and a full set of conversion tables for everything from tyre pressures to shoe sizes. Bon voyage!

A Word of Advice

This book has been planned to make everything as easy to find as possible, but so that you won't have to fumble when you want a phrase in a hurry, try to read it through before you go away. There's no need to try and learn anything: just remember where the various sections come in the book. It will often be a good idea to look up a key word in the index, and this will take you to what you want to say.

FIRST THINGS FIRST
How To Pronounce French

We've tried to make the pronunciation aids under the phrases as clear as possible, but English spelling isn't enough to give a true idea of how French sounds – you can only get that by listening to the French. Here we just want to give you a little advice about some sounds that English-speakers often find troublesome.

In English, *r*'s are often ignored, so that *sore* and *saw* sound the same. Not so in French. In a word like *bar* it has to be properly pronounced, rolled slightly at the back of the mouth.

Some French sounds are quite different from any you hear in English, like the vowel in *rue (rōō)*, which many people can't distinguish from the one in *roue (roo)*. To make it you have to purse your lips and then try to say *ee*.

French also has nasal vowels, vowels followed by the letter *n: an, en, ain* etc. You sometimes hear this sort of sound at the end of the word *restaurant*. You make these sounds by breathing out slightly through the nose as you pronounce the vowel shown in the pronunciation. Again many people cannot make the distinction between the sounds in *banc* and *bon*, so we've cheated and just used *oñ* to represent them both. To be absolutely correct you should pronounce *an* and *en* further back in the mouth than *on*.

The letter *e* in French often has a very weak sound, rather like the one written *a* in *above* or *o* in *position*. We've shown this as *uh*.

The letters *zh* may look odd, but they stand for a common sound written with an *s* in English in words like *television* and *measure*.

Remember that the pronunciations have to be taken at face value, or you may be led astray by English spellings which can be pronounced in more than one way. Don't confuse *s* with *z* or *e* with *ee*: *service* is *ser-vees* not *ser-veez* and *après* is *a-pre* not *a-pree*. Be very careful when a pronunciation looks like an actual English word: for instance *poste* is shown as *post*, but it has to rhyme with *lost* not *most!*

How To Pronounce French

French spelling	Closest English sound		Shown here by	Example	
ch		ship	sh	chat	sha
ç		sat	s	façon	fa-soñ
g	before	a, o, u, got	g	gateau	ga-tō
	before	e, ı, measure	zh	rouge	roozh
gn		companion	ny	vigne	veen-yuh
h		not pronounced		homme	om
j		measure	zh	joue	zhoo
qu		kick	k	quel	kel
r		carrot (see note)	r	rouge	roozh
w		vase	v	wagon	va-goñ
a, â		father	ah	plage	plahzh
a, à		fat	a	chat	sha
ai		play	ay	quai	kay
	or	set	e	mais	me
ail		buy	ye	travail	tra-vye
au, eau		boat	ō	faux	fō
e, è		set	e	mets	me
é		play	ay	été	ay-tay
eu		thud	uh	pleut	pluh
i		meet	ee	vide	veed
o	British	pot, US thought	o	bol	bol
	or	boat	ō	trop	trō
oi	British	suave	wah	mois	mwah
ou		boot	oo	bout	boo
u		see note	ōō	rue	rōō
y		meet	ee	cycle	see-kluh
an, en etc.		see note	oñ etc	plan	ploñ

Everyday Phrases

To start off, a few phrases you can use for basic contact with the Frenchman in the street.

Good morning	– Bonjour	Monsieur *(to a man)*
Good afternoon	*boñ-zhoor*	*muhs-yuh*
		Madame *(to a woman)*
		ma-dam
		Mademoiselle *(to a girl)*
		mad-mwah-zel

Good evening – Bonsoir
boñ-swar

Good night – Bonne nuit
bon nwee

Goodbye – Au revoir
ō ruh-vwar

Yes – Oui
wee

No – Non
noñ

How are you? – Comment allez-vous?
ko-moñ tal-ay voo?

I'm very well – Très bien, merci
tre byeñ mer-see

Please – S'il vous plaît
see voo play

Yes please – Oui merci
wee mer-see

Thank you – Merci
mer-see

No thank you – Non merci
noñ mer-see

That's very kind of you – C'est très gentil à vous
say tre zhoñ-tee a voo

You're welcome – Je vous en prie
zhuh voo zoñ pree

Everyday Phrases

I'm sorry – Pardon
par-doñ

Excuse me – Excusez-moi
ex-kōō-zay mwah

It doesn't matter – Ça ne fait rien
sa nuh fe ryeñ

I don't mind – Ça m'est égal
sa met ay-gal

My name is Mark Roberts – Je m'appelle Mark Roberts
zhuh ma-pel Mark Roberts

What is your name? – Comment vous appelez-vous?
ko-moñ voo za-play voo?

I come from America – Je suis américain
zhuh swee za-may-ree-kañ

I come from Britain – Je suis britannique
zhuh swee bree-ta-neek

I live in Chester – J'habite à Chester
zha-beet a Chester

I am on holiday (vacation) – Je suis en vacances
zhuh swee zoñ va-koñs

See you soon – À bientôt
a byeñ-tō

Your First Questions

You won't go very far before you want to ask questions like these.
We may not have given the exact question you need, and you may
have to change a few words, but you should manage. The key part of
some very common questions is in capitals; you can vary the ending
yourself as circumstances require.

I WANT a single room — JE VOUDRAIS une chambre pour une
personne
zhuh voo-dre zōōn shoñ-bruh poor ōōn per-son

**WE WANT to buy some
souvenirs** — NOUS VOULONS acheter des
souvenirs
noo voo-loñ zash-tay day soov-neer

How much does that cost? — Combien ça coûte?
koñ-byeñ sa koot?

I WANT to make a phone call — JE VOUDRAIS téléphoner
zhuh voo-dre tay-lay-fō-nay

I NEED a doctor — IL ME FAUT un docteur
eel muh fō tuñ dok-tur

**WHERE IS the Tourist
Information Office?** — OÙ EST le syndicat d'initiative?
oo ay luh sañ-dee-ka deen-ee-sya-teev?

**WE ARE LOOKING FOR a
camping site** — NOUS CHERCHONS un camping
noo sher-shoñ zuñ koñ-peeng

**DO YOU KNOW a good
restaurant?** — EST-CE QUE VOUS CONNAISSEZ
un bon restaurant?
es-kuh voo ko-nay-say uñ boñ res-tō-roñ?

SHOULD WE reserve a table? — EST-CE QUE NOUS DEVRIONS
réserver une table?
*es-kuh noo duh-vree-oñ ray-zer-vay ōōn
ta-bluh?*

**HOW LONG WILL IT TAKE
TO repair the car?** — IL FAUDRA COMBIEN DE TEMPS
POUR réparer la voiture?
*eel fō-dra koñ-byeñ duh toñ poor ray-pa-ray la
vwah-tōōr?*

Your First Questions

CAN I rent a car? – EST-CE QUE JE PEUX louer une voiture?
es-kuh zhuh puh loo-ay ōōn vwah-tōōr?

What time is it please? – Quelle heure est-il s'il vous plaît?
kel ur et-eel see voo play?

WHEN IS THE NEXT TRAIN to Nice? – À QUELLE HEURE EST LE PROCHAIN TRAIN pour Nice?
a kel ur ay luh pro-shañ trañ poor nees?

WHAT TIME do you close? – Vous fermez À QUELLE HEURE?
voo fer-may a kel ur?

MAY I BORROW your pen? – EST-CE QUE JE PEUX EMPRUNTER votre stylo?
es-kuh zhuh puh zoñ-pruñ-tay vo-truh stee-lō?

DO I HAVE TIME TO buy a magazine? – EST-CE QUE J'AI LE TEMPS d'acheter un magazine?
es-kuh zhay luh toñ dash-tay uñ ma-gaz-een?

What is this? – Qu'est-ce que c'est?
kes-kuh say?

Who did this? – Qui a fait ça?
kee a fe sa?

Who should I see about this? – Je dois m'adresser à qui, pour ça?
zhuh dwah ma-dre-say a kee poor sa?

HAVE YOU GOT any matches? – EST-CE QUE VOUS AVEZ des allumettes?
es-kuh voo zav-ay day za-lōō-met?

Do you mind if I . . . ? – Vous permettez . . . ?
voo per-me-tay . . . ?

Problems

Of course we hope you won't have any, and that if you do they're minor ones and not real emergencies. The phrases we've given below cover both and are meant to help you through any difficulties that may come along.

Can you help me please?	– Est-ce que vous pouvez m'aider, s'il vous plaît?
	es-kuh voo poo-vay may-day, see voo play?
Could you come with me please?	– Est-ce que vous pouvez venir avec moi, s'il vous plaît?
	es-kuh voo poo-vay vuh-neer a-vek mwah, see voo play?
What's the matter?	– Qu'est-ce qu'il y a?
	kes-keel-ya?
What do you think is wrong?	– Qu'est-ce qui ne va pas?
	kes-kee nuh va pa?
I don't understand	– Je ne comprends pas
	zhuh nuh koñ-proñ pa
I don't speak French	– Je ne parle pas français
	zhuh nuh parl pa froñ-se
Please repeat that	– Répétez, s'il vous plaît
	ray-pay-tay, see voo play
I need someone who speaks English	– J'ai besoin de quelqu'un qui parle anglais
	zhay buh-zwañ duh kel-kuñ kee parl oñ-glay
I haven't enough money	– Je n'ai pas assez d'argent
	zhuh nay pa za-say dar-zhoñ
I have no money	– Je n'ai pas d'argent
	zhuh nay pa dar-zhoñ
Is there somewhere open where we can eat?	– Est-ce qu'on peut manger quelque part maintenant?
	es-koñ puh moñ-zhay kel-kuh par mañt-noñ?
That man keeps following me	– Cet homme me suit sans arrêt
	set om muh swee soñ za-re

Problems

Stop following me	Arrêtez de me suivre *a-re-tay duh muh swee-vruh*
Call the police	Appelez la police *a-play la po-lees*
My car has been broken into	On s'est introduit dans ma voiture par effraction *oñ set añ-tro-dwee doñ ma vwah-tōōr par e-frax-yoñ*
My son is lost	Mon fils a disparu *moñ fees a dees-pa-rōō*
Where is the police station?	Où est le poste de police? *oo ay luh post duh po-lees?*
I have lost my passport	J'ai perdu mon passeport *zhay per-dōō moñ pas-por*
My wallet has been stolen	On a volé mon portefeuille *oñ a vo-lay moñ por-tuh-fye*
The insurance company requires me to report it	Ma compagnie d'assurance exige que la police soit informée *ma koñ-pan-yee da-sōō-roñs eg-zeezh kuh la po-lees swa tañ-for-may*
I want to see a lawyer	Je demande à voir un avocat *zhuh duh-moñd a vwar uñ na-vō-ka*
Please give me my passport back	Mon passeport, s'il vous plaît *moñ pas-por, see voo play*
Where is the British Consulate?	Où est le Consulat britannique? *oo ay luh koñ-sōō-la bree-ta-neek?*
There is a fire	Il y a le feu *eel ee a luh fuh*
There has been an accident	Il y a un accident *eel ee a uñ ax-ee-doñ*
Call an ambulance	Appelez une ambulance *a-play zōōn oñ-bōō-loñs*

Problems

I need a doctor	– Il me faut un docteur *eel muh fō tuñ dok-tur*
I feel ill	– Je ne me sens pas bien *zhuh nuh muh soñ pa byeñ*
He has hurt himself	– Il s'est blessé *eel say ble-say*
My car won't start	– Ma voiture ne veut pas démarrer *ma vwah-tōōr nuh vuh pa day-ma-ray*
There is something wrong with the brakes	– Les freins marchent mal *lay frañ marsh mal*
This is broken	– C'est cassé *say ka-say*
The air-conditioning does not work	– L'air conditionné ne marche pas *ler koñ-dee-syo-nay nuh marsh pa*
I am in a hurry	– Je suis pressé *zhuh swee pre-say*
How long will this take?	– Combien de temps est-ce que cela prendra? *koñ-byeñ duh toñ es-kuh sla proñ-dra?*
How long will the delay be?	– Il y aura un retard de combien de temps? *eel yō-ra uñ ruh-tar duh koñ-byeñ duh toñ?*
I am leaving tomorrow. Can you do it at once?	– Je pars demain. Est-ce que vous pouvez me faire ça immédiatement? *zhuh par duh-mañ. es-kuh voo poo-vay muh fer sa ee-mayd-yat-moñ?*
I have forgotten my glasses	– J'ai oublié mes lunettes *zhay oo-blee-ay may lōō-net*
I have left my bag in the toilet (restroom)	– J'ai laissé mon sac dans les toilettes *zhay lay-say moñ sak doñ lay twah-let*
My luggage has not arrived	– Mes bagages ne sont pas arrivés *may ba-gazh nuh soñ pa za-ree-vay*
I have missed my train	– J'ai manqué mon train *zhay moñ-kay moñ trañ*

Problems

The people who who were to meet me have not turned up — Les personnes que je devais rencontrer ne sont pas venues
lay per-son kuh zhuh duh-ve roñ-koñ-tray nuh soñ pa vuh-nōō

My party has left without me — Mon groupe est parti sans moi
moñ groop ay par-tee soñ mwah

I have lost my way. How do I get to the station? — Je me suis perdu. Où est la gare?
zhuh muh swee per-dōō. oo ay la gar?

I have broken a glass — J'ai cassé un verre
zhay ka-say uñ ver

I have spilt something — J'ai renversé quelque chose
zhay roñ-ver-say kel-kuh-shōz

My clothes are soaked. Where can I dry them? — Mes vêtements sont trempés. Où est-ce que je peux les faire sécher?
may vet-moñ soñ troñ-pay. oo es-kuh zhuh puh lay fer say-shay?

When You Arrive
The Formalities

Entering France is usually a simple business. You may possibly be stopped and asked a few questions – the answers given here should be adequate. The two customs channels are red (*objets à déclarer*) for dutiable goods, and green (*rien à déclarer*) if you have nothing to declare. Check duty-free allowances before you go as they may change from time to time.

Here is my passport – Voici mon passeport
vwah-see moñ pas-por

My wife and I are on a joint passport – Ma femme et moi sommes sur le même passeport
ma fam ay mwah som soōr luh mem pas-por

Our children are on this passport – Nos enfants sont sur ce passeport
nō zoñ-foñ soñ soōr suh pas-por

Here is my driving licence and green card – Voici mon permis de conduire et la carte verte
vwah-see moñ per-mee duh koñ-dweer ay la kart vert

I am staying for 2 weeks – Je reste deux semaines
zhuh rest duh smen

We are visiting some friends – Nous allons voir des amis
noo zal-oñ vwar day za-mee

I have nothing to declare – Je n'ai rien à déclarer
zhuh nay ryeñ a day-kla-ray

I have the usual allowances of cigarettes and spirits (liquor) – J'ai le nombre de cigarettes et de bouteilles permises
zhay luh noñ-bruh duh see-ga-ret ay duh boo-tay per-meez

That is for my personal use – C'est pour ma consommation personnelle
say poor ma koñ-so-mas-yoñ per-so-nel

How much do I have to pay? – C'est combien?
say koñ-byeñ?

Is that all? – C'est tout?
say too?

When You Arrive
Your Luggage

Where do I get the connecting flight to Marseille? — Où est la correspondance pour Marseille?
oo ay la ko-res-poñ-doñs poor mar-say?

Where do I get the Paris train? — Où est le train de Paris?
oo ay luh trañ duh pa-ree?

Is there a bus into town? — Est-ce qu'il y a un car pour le centre-ville?
es-keel ya uñ kar poor luh soñ-truh-veel?

Where is the luggage from the London flight? — Où sont les bagages du vol de Londres?
oo soñ lay ba-gazh dōō vol duh loñ-druh?

My suitcase is stuck on the conveyor belt — Ma valise est bloquée sur le tapis roulant
ma va-leez ay blo-kay sōōr luh ta-pee roo-loñ

Are there any porters? — Est-ce qu'il y a des porteurs?
es-keel ee a day por-tur?

Are there any luggage trolleys (carriers)? — Est-ce qu'il y a des chariots à bagages?
es-keel ee a day shar-yō a ba-gazh?

Is there any charge? — Est-ce qu'il faut payer quelque chose?
es-keel fō pay-ay kel-kuh-shōz?

Is there a left-luggage office (baggage room)? — Est-ce qu'il y a une consigne?
es-keel ee a ōōn koñ-seen-yuh?

Please take these bags to a taxi — Portez ces valises jusqu'à un taxi, s'il vous plaît
por-tay say va-leez zhōō-ska uñ tax-ee, see voo play

I'll carry that myself, thank you — Je peux porter ça moi-même, merci
zhuh puh por-tay sa mwah-mem, mer-see

Careful, the handle is broken — Attention, la poignée est cassée
a-toñ-syoñ, la pwahn-yay ay kas-ay

No, don't put that on top! — Non, ne mettez pas ça dessus!
noñ, nuh me-tay pa sa duh-sōō!

That bag is not mine — Ça, ce n'est pas ma valise
sa, snay pa ma va-leez

Where is my other bag? — Où est mon autre valise?
oo ay mo nō-truh va-leez?

Asking The Way
Things You'll Hear

It's no use being able to ask the way if you're not going to understand the directions you get. We've tried to anticipate the likely answers, so listen carefully for these key phrases:

Vous allez – **tout droit**
voo za-lay　*too drwah*
You go　straight ahead

– **à droite**
a drwaht
right

– **à gauche**
a gōsh
left

– **jusqu'à**
zhōos-ka
as far as

Tournez – **à droite**
toor-nay　*a drwaht*
Turn　right

– **à gauche**
a gōsh
left

Continuez – **vers**
koñ-tee-nōo-ay　*ver*
Keep going straight ahead　towards

– **jusqu'à ce que**
zhōos-kas kuh
until

Prenez – **la direction de . . .**
pruh-nay　*la dee-rex-yoñ duh . . .*
Take　the road for . . .

– **la première à droite**
la pruhm-yer a drwaht
the first (road) on the right

– **la deuxième à gauche**
la duh-zyem a gōsh
the second (road) on the left

Asking the Way
Things You'll Hear

Traversez – **la rue**
tra-ver-say   *la rōō*
Cross   the street

– **la place**
la plas
the square

Passez – **le passage à niveau**
pa-say   *luh pa-sazh a nee-vō*
Cross over   the level crossing

– **le pont**
luh poñ
the bridge

C'est – **tout près d'ici**
say   *too pre dee-see*
It's   not far from here

– **au croisement**
tō krwahz-moñ
at the junction (intersection)

– **à côté du théâtre**
ta kō-tay dōō tay-ah-truh
next to the theatre

– **après les feux**
ta-pre lay fuh
after the traffic lights

– **en face de l'église**
toñ fas duh lay-gleez
opposite the church

– **par là**
par la
over there

– **au coin de la rue**
tō kwañ duh la rōō
at the corner

Asking the Way

The simplest way to get directions is just to say where you want to go.

Where is the cathedral? – La cathédrale s'il vous plaît?
la ka-tay-dral see voo play?

Can you tell me the way to the airport? – L'aéroport, s'il vous plaît?
ler-ō-por see voo play?

But otherwise –

Where is the exit? – Où est la sortie?
oo ay la sor-tee?

Where are the toilets? – Où sont les toilettes?
oo soñ lay twah-let?

Can you tell me the way to the station? – Pouvez-vous m'indiquer le chemin de la gare?
poo-vay voo mañ-dee-kay luh shmañ duh la gar?

Where is the nearest post office? – Où est la poste la plus proche?
oo ay la post la plōō prosh?

Is there a service station near here? – Est-ce qu'il y a une station-service dans les environs?
es-keel ya ōōn stas-yoñ-ser-vees doñ lay zoñ-vee-roñ?

Is this the right way to the castle? – Est-ce que c'est le chemin pour aller au château?
es-kuh say luh shmañ poor a-lay ō sha-tō?

How long will it take to get there? – Combien de temps faut-il pour y aller?
koñ-byeñ duh toñ fō-teel poor ee a-lay?

Is it far? – Est-ce que c'est loin?
es-kuh say lwañ?

Is it far to Montmartre? – Est-ce que c'est loin, Montmartre?
es-kuh say lwañ, moñ-mar-truh?

Can you walk there? – Est-ce qu'on peut y aller à pied?
es-koñ puh tee a-lay a pyay?

Is there a bus that goes there? – Est-ce qu'il y a un bus pour y aller?
es-keel ya uñ bōōs poor ee a-lay?

Where is the nearest hospital?. – Où est l'hôpital le plus proche?
oo ay lo-pee-tal luh plōō prosh?

I have lost my way – Je suis perdu
zhuh swee per-dōō

I am trying to get to the centre of the city – Je voudrais aller au centre-ville
zhuh voo-dre za-lay ō soñ-truh-veel

I am looking for the Tourist Information Office – Je cherche le syndicat d'initiative
zhuh shersh luh sañ-dee-ka dee-nee-sya-teev

Can you show me on the map? – Est-ce que vous pouvez me montrer sur la carte?
es-kuh voo poo-vay muh moñ-tray sōōr la kart?

Which road do I take for Bordeaux? – Je prends quelle route pour Bordeaux?
zhuh proñ kel root poor bor-dō?

How far is it to Brussels? – Bruxelles est à quelle distance?
brōō-sèl et a kel dee-stoñs?

Will we arrive by this evening? – Est-ce que nous arriverons avant ce soir?
es-kuh noo za-ree-vuh-roñ a-voñ suh swar?

Which is the best route to Nîmes? – Quelle est la meilleure route pour aller à Nîmes?
kel ay la may-yur root poor a-lay a neem?

Which is the most scenic route? – Quelle est la route la plus pittoresque?
kel ay la root la plōō pee-to-resk?

Do I turn here for Nîmes? – Est-ce que je tourne ici pour Nîmes?
es-kuh zhuh toorn ee-see poor neem?

Is the traffic one-way? – Est-ce qu'il y a un système de sens uniques?
es-keel ya uñ see-stem duh soñ sōō-neek?

How do I get onto the road for Arles? – Je rejoins la route d'Arles comment?
zhuh ruh-zhwañ la root darl ko-moñ?

How do I get onto the motorway (highway)? – Je rejoins l'autoroute comment?
zhuh ruh-zhwañ lō-tō-root ko-moñ?

Where does this road go to? – Où va cette route?
oo va set root?

Buses & Metro

In most cities you'll find a pay-as-you-enter bus system. Paris has the metro, along with Lyon, and one ticket will take you wherever you want to go. Tickets can be bought singly, but it is far more economical to buy them in tens; you should ask for *un carnet*. They are also used on the Paris bus network, but you will need more than one ticket for longer journeys; 4 and 7 day runabout tickets *(billets touristiques)* are also available for both buses and metro.

Which bus do I take for the Louvre? – Quel est le bus qui passe au Louvre?
kel ay luh bōōs kee pas ō loo-vruh?

Where do I get a bus for Orly? – Où est-ce que je prends le car qui va à Orly?
oo es-kuh zhuh proñ luh kar kee va a or-lee?

Does this bus go to the Opéra? – Est-ce que ce bus va à l'Opéra?
es-kuh suh bōōs va a lo-pay-rah?

Where should I change? – Je dois changer où?
zhuh dwah shoñ-zhay oo?

I want to go to Notre Dame – Je veux aller à Notre Dame
zhuh vuh zal-ay a not-ruh dam

How many tickets do I need? – Je dois poinçonner combien de tickets?
zhuh dwah pwañ-so-nay koñ-byeñ duh tee-kay?

A 7-day tourist ticket please – Un billet touristique pour sept jours s'il vous plaît
uñ bee-yay too-ree-steek poor set zhoor see voo play

Will you let me off at the right stop? – Est-ce que vous pouvez me dire où descendre?
es-kuh voo poo-vay muh deer oo de-soñ-druh?

What is the fare to the centre of the city? – Combien ça coûte jusqu'au centre-ville?
koñ-byeñ sa koot zhōō-skō soñ-truh-veel?

When is the last bus? – Le dernier bus est à quelle heure?
luh dern-yay bōōs et a kel ur?

How long does it take to get to the Odéon? – Est-ce long pour aller à l'Odéon?
es loñ poor a-lay a lō-day-oñ?

Taxis can be picked up at a rank or hailed: they may not stop if they are too close to a stand. A tip of a few francs is expected.

The Gare du Nord please – La gare du Nord, s'il vous plaît
la gar dōō nor see voo play

30, avenue des Dames please – Trente avenue des Dames, s'il vous plaît
troñt av-nōō day dam see voo play

Please take me to this address – Conduisez-moi à cette adresse, s'il vous plaît
koñ-dwee-zay mwah a set a-dres see voo play

Take me to the airport please – Conduisez-moi à l'aéroport, s'il vous plaît
koñ-dwee-zay mwah a ler-ō-por see voo play

Will you put the luggage in the boot (trunk)? – Est-ce que vous pouvez mettre ces bagages dans le coffre?
es-kuh voo poo-vay met-ruh say ba-gazh doñ luh kof-ruh?

Please drive us around the town – Faites-nous faire un petit tour dans la ville s'il vous plaît
fet noo fer uñ puh-tee toor doñ la veel see voo play

I'm in a hurry – Je suis pressé
zhuh swee pre-say

Please wait here for a few minutes – Attendez ici quelques minutes s'il vous plaît
a-toñ-day zee-see kel-kuh mee-nōōt see voo play

Turn left please – Tournez à gauche s'il vous plaît
toor-nay za gōsh see voo play

Turn right please – Tournez à droite s'il vous plaît
toor-nay za drwaht see voo play

Please stop at the corner – Arrêtez au coin de la rue s'il vous plaît
a-ret-ay ō kwañ duh la rōō see voo play

How much is that please? – C'est combien, s'il vous plaît?
say koñ-byeñ, see voo play?

Keep the change – Gardez la monnaie
gar-day la mo-nay

Trains
Your Ticket

The trains you're most likely to travel on are those between Calais, Boulogne and Paris, which can be rather full. But the railways do provide an excellent way of seeing France. An extra charge is payable on some express trains or *rapides* (remember *un express* is an ordinary fast train); children under ten travel half-fare and those under four travel free.

You will see the sign –

N'OUBLIEZ PAS DE COMPOSTER VOTRE BILLET

"Do not forget to cancel your ticket." You should insert it in the machine at the platform entrance. Forgetting could mean an on-the-spot fine from a ticket inspector!

If you travel at night you can reserve either a sleeper or a couchette, which is a simple berth with blankets in a compartment shared by several passengers.

A single (one-way ticket) to Nice please	– Un aller simple pour Nice s'il vous plaît *uñ na-lay sañ-pluh poor nees see voo play*
A return (round-trip ticket) to Nice please	– Un aller-retour pour Nice s'il vous plaît *uñ na-lay ruh-toor poor nees see voo play*
A return to Nice, first class	– Un aller-retour pour Nice en première *uñ na-lay ruh-toor poor nees oñ pruh-myer*
A child's return to Nice	– Un aller-retour enfant pour Nice *uñ na-lay ruh-toor oñ-foñ poor nees*
He is under ten	– Il a moins de dix ans *eel a mwañ duh dee zoñ*
When is the next train to Tours?	– Le prochain train pour Tours part à quelle heure? *luh pro-shañ trañ poor toor par ta kel ur?*
What are the times of trains to Tours?	– Quels sont les horaires des trains pour Tours? *kel soñ lay zo-rer day trañ poor toor?*
What time is the last train to Tours?	– Le dernier train pour Tours est à quelle heure? *luh dern-yay trañ poor toor et a kel ur?*

Trains
Your Ticket

I want to book a seat on the 1030 to Calais
— Je voudrais réserver une place dans le train de Calais de 10.30
zhuh voo-dre ray-zer-vay ōōn plas doñ luh trañ duh ka-lay duh dee zur troñt

Second class, by the window
— Un billet de deuxième classe, près de la fenêtre
uñ bee-yay duh duh-zyem klas, pre duh la fnet-ruh

First class, in a smoking compartment
— Première classe dans un compartiment pour fumeurs
pruh-myer klas doñ zuñ koñ-par-tee-moñ poor fōō-mur

A no-smoking compartment please
— Un compartiment pour non-fumeurs, s'il vous plaît
uñ koñ-par-tee-moñ poor noñ fōō-mur see voo play

Can I have a sleeper on the 2200 to Lyon?
— Je voudrais un wagon-lit dans le train de Lyon de 22 heures
zhuh voo-dre zuñ va-goñ-lee doñ luh trañ duh lee-yoñ duh vañ-duh zūr

Can I have a couchette on the 2200 to Lyon?
— Je voudrais une couchette dans le train de Lyon de 22 heures
zhuh voo-dre zōōn koo-shet doñ luh trañ duh lee-yoñ duh vañ-duh zur

Where is the departure board (listing)?
— Où est le tableau des départs?
oo ay luh ta-blō day day-par?

I want to send this suitcase in advance
— Je voudrais faire partir cette valise en bagages accompagnés
zhuh voo-dre fer par-teer set va-leez oñ ba-gazh a-koñ-pan-yay

I sent a suitcase in advance. Where do I pick it up?
— J'ai fait partir une valise en bagages accompagnés. Où est-ce que je la récupère?
zhay fay par-teer ōōn va-leez oñ ba-gazh a-koñ-pan-yay. oo es-kuh zhuh la ray-kōō-per?

Trains
In the Station

I want to leave these bags in the left luggage (baggage room) – Je désire laisser ces valises à la consigne
zhuh day-zeer lay-say say va-leez a la koñ-seen-yuh

I shall pick them up this evening – Je les reprendrai ce soir
zhuh lay ruh-proñ-dray suh swar

What time do you close? – Vous fermez à quelle heure?
voo fer-may za kel ur?

How much is it per suitcase? – C'est combien par valise?
say koñ-byeñ par va-leez?

Please take these bags to platform 9 – Portez ces valises jusqu'au quai neuf, s'il vous plaît
por-tay say va-leez zhōō-skō kay nuhf see voo play

Would you look after these bags for a minute please? – Est-ce que vous pourriez garder ces valises une minute s'il vous plaît?
es-kuh voo poo-ree-ay gar-day say va-leez ōōn mee-nōōt see voo play?

What platform do I go to for the Nice train? – Le train pour Nice part de quel quai?
luh trañ poor nees par duh kel kay?

Is this the right platform for Nice? – Est-ce que c'est le bon quai pour Nice?
es-kuh say luh boñ kay poor nees?

Is this the Nice train? – Est-ce que c'est bien le train pour Nice?
es-kuh say byeñ luh trañ poor nees?

What time does the train leave? – Le train part à quelle heure?
luh trañ par ta kel ur?

Is there a dining car? – Est-ce qu'il y a un wagon-restaurant?
es-keel ya uñ va-goñ res-tō-roñ?

Is there a buffet (club) car? – Est-ce qu'il y a un buffet?
es-keel ya uñ bōō-fe?

What time do we get to Nice? – Nous arrivons à Nice à quelle heure?
noo za-ree-voñ a nees a kel ur?

Do we stop at Lyon? – Est-ce que nous nous arrêtons à Lyon?
es-kuh noo noo za-re-toñ a lee-yoñ?

Is this a through train? – Est-ce que c'est un train direct?
es-kuh set uñ trañ dee-rekt?

Trains
In the train

Where do I have to change for Toulon? – Où faut-il changer pour Toulon?
oo fō-teel shoñ-zhay poor too-loñ?

How long do I have before my next train leaves? – Je dois attendre la correspondance combien de temps?
zhuh dwah zat-oñ-druh la ko-res-poñ-doñs koñ-byeñ duh toñ?

Is this seat free? – Est-ce que cette place est libre?
es-kuh set plas ay lee-bruh?

This is my seat – Ceci, c'est ma place
suh-see, say ma plas

Can you help me with my bags please? – Est-ce que vous pouvez m'aider avec mes valises, s'il vous plaît?
es-kuh voo poo-vay may-day a-vek may va-leez see voo play?

May I open the window? – Est-ce que je peux ouvrir la fenêtre?
es-kuh zhuh puh zoo-vreer la fue-truh?

This is a no-smoking compartment – Ceci est un compartiment pour non-fumeurs
suh-see et uñ koñ-par-tee-moñ poor noñ fōo-mur

My wife has my ticket – Ma femme a mon billet
ma fam a moñ bee-yay

Are we at Lyon yet? – Est-ce que nous sommes déjà à Lyon?
es-kuh noo som day-zha a lee-yoñ?

Are we on time? – Est-ce que nous sommes à l'heure?
es-kuh noo som za lur?

Driving
Service Station

L'essence – petrol or gas – comes in two varieties in France:
ordinaire (= 2 star) and *super* (= 4 star). We've set out conversion
tables on page 117 for you to work out how many litres to ask for,
and to tell you what your metric tyre pressure should be.

15 litres of – **2 star**
Quinze litres d'ordinaire
kañz lee-truh *dor-dee-ner*

– **4 star**
de super
duh sōō-per

– **diesel fuel**
de diesel
duh dee-zel

50 francs worth please – Pour cinquante francs s'il vous plaît
poor sañ-koñt froñ see voo play

Fill her up please – Le plein s'il vous plaît
luh plañ see voo play

Check – **the oil**
Vérifiez l'huile
vay-reef-yay *lweel*

– **the water**
l'eau
lō

I want some distilled water – Je voudrais de l'eau distillée
zhuh voo-dre duh lō dee-stee-yay

Check the tyre pressure – Vérifiez la pression des pneus, s'il vous
please plaît
vay-reef-yay la pres-yoñ day pnuh see voo play

The pressure is 1.3 – La pression est de un virgule trois
la pres-yoñ ay duh uñ veer-gōōl trwah

Could you clean the – Faites le pare-brise s'il vous plaît
windscreen (windshield)? *fet luh par-breez see voo play*

Could you put some water in – Remplissez le lave-glace s'il vous plaît
the windscreen washer? *roñ-plee-say luh lav-glas see voo play*

Driving
Parking

Sad to say, disc zones in towns, where you just leave a parking disc by your windscreen, showing the time you arrived and when you should leave, are giving way to parking meters. The traffic wardens in Paris are easily recognisable in their tasteful blue uniforms. Away from town centres there are streets where parking is allowed only on one side on a given day, for example during the first half of the month or on odd-numbered dates.

Can I park here? – Est-ce que je peux me garer ici?
es-kuh zhuh puh muh ga-ray ee-see?

Is there a car park (parking lot) nearby? – Est-ce qu'il y a un parking près d'ici?
es-keel ya uñ par-keeng pre dee-see?

Do I need a parking disc? – Est-ce que le disque de stationnement est obligatoire?
es-kuh luh deesk duh stas-yon-moñ et ob-lee-ga-twar?

Where can I get a parking disc? – Où trouve-t-on les disques de stationnement?
oo troov toñ lay deesk duh stas-yon-moñ?

Do I need parking lights? – Est-ce que les feux de position sont nécessaires?
es-kuh lay fuh duh poz-ees-yoñ soñ nay-se-ser?

What time does the car park close? – Le parking ferme à quelle heure?
luh par-keeng ferm a kel ur?

How long can I stay here? – Je peux rester ici combien de temps?
zhuh puh res-tay ee-see koñ-byeñ duh toñ?

Can I park on this side today? – Est-ce que le stationnement est autorisé de ce côté aujourd'hui?
es-kuh luh stas-yon-moñ et ō-to-ree-zay duh suh kō-tay ō-zhoor-dwee?

Driving
Road Conditions

French roads are usually very good. The only problems you're likely to meet are peak traffic in summer, or heavy snow if you're off on a winter sports trip. The traffic authorities signpost alternative routes on minor roads with green arrows (*les flèches vertes*), and in winter studded snow-tyres or chains may be compulsory.

WARNING! Pay attention to those *Priorité à droite* signs! Traffic from the right always has right of way unless you see a sign saying *Passage protégé* Both signs are shown inside the back cover of this book.

Is the traffic heavy?	Est-ce que les routes sont encombrées?
	es-kuh lay root soñ toñ-koñ-bray?
Are there any hold-ups (tie-ups)?	Est-ce qu'il y a des bouchons?
	es-keel ya day boo-shoñ?
What's causing this hold-up?	Ce bouchon est provoqué par quoi?
	suh boo-shoñ ay pro-vo-kay par kwah?
When will the road be clear?	La route sera dégagée quand?
	la root suh-ra day-ga-zhay koñ?
Is there a detour?	Est-ce qu'il y a une déviation?
	es-keel ya ōn day-vyas-yoñ?
What is the speed limit?	La vitesse est limitée à combien?
	la vee-tes ay lee-mee-tay a koñ-byeñ?
Is there a toll on this motorway (highway)?	Est-ce qu'il y a un péage sur cette autoroute?
	es-keel ya uñ pay-yazh sōōr set ō-tō-root?
Is the road to Chamonix snowed up?	Est-ce que la route de Chamonix est enneigée?
	es-kuh la root duh sha-mo-nee et oñ-nezh-ay?
Is the pass open?	Est-ce que le col est ouvert?
	es-kuh luh kol et oo-ver?
Do I need studded tyres?	Est-ce qu'il faut des pneus à clous?
	es-keel fō day pnuh a kloo?
Do I need chains?	Est-ce qu'il faut des chaînes?
	es-keel fō day shen?

Driving
Renting a Car

I want to rent a car	– Je désire louer une voiture *zhuh day-zeer loo-ay ōōn vwah-tōōr*
I want it for 5 days	– Je la voudrais pour cinq jours *zhuh la voo-dre poor sañk zhoor*
Is mileage included?	– Est-ce que le kilométrage est compris? *es-kuh luh kee-lō-me-trazh et koñ-pree?*
Have you got Est-ce que vous avez *es-kuh voo za-vay*	**– a larger car?** une voiture plus grande? *zōōn vwah-tōōr plōō groñd?*
	– a cheaper car? une voiture moins chère? *zōōn vwah-tōōr mwañ sher?*
	– an automatic? une voiture automatique? *zōōn vwah-tōōr ō-tō-ma-teek?*
My wife will be driving as well	– Ma femme conduira aussi *ma fam koñ-dwee-ra ō-see*
Must I return the car here?	– Est-ce qu'il faut rapporter la voiture ici? *es-keel fō ra-por-tay la vwah-tōōr ee-see?*
I would like to leave the car in Nice	– Je voudrais laisser la voiture à Nice *zhuh voo-dre lay-say la vwah-tōōr a nees*
Please show me how to operate Montrez-moi comment marchent *moñ-tray mwah ko-moñ marsh*	**– the lights** les phares *lay far*
	–– the windscreen wipers les essuie-glace *lay zes-wee-glas*
Where is reverse?	– Où est la marche arrière? *oo ay la marsh a-ree-yer?*
Please explain the car documents	– Expliquez-moi s'il vous plaît les différents papiers de la voiture *ex-plee-kay mwah see voo play lay dee-fay-roñ* *pap-yay duh la vwah-tōōr*

Driving
Breakdowns & Repairs

I have had a breakdown – Ma voiture est en panne
ma vwah-tōōr et oñ pan

Can you send – **a mechanic?**
Est-ce que vous pouvez envoyer un mécanicien?
es-kuh voo poo-vay zoñ-vwah-yay *uñ may-ka-nees-yeñ?*

– **a breakdown van (tow-truck)?**
une dépanneuse?
ōōn day-pa-nuhz?

Can you take me to the nearest – Est-ce que vous pouvez m'emmener au
garage? garage le plus proche?
es-kuh voo poo-vay mom-nay ō ga-razh luh plōō prosh?

Can you give me a tow? – Est-ce que vous pouvez me remorquer?
es-kuh voo poo-vay muh ruh-mor-kay?

I have run out of petrol (gas) – Je suis en panne d'essence
zhuh swee zoñ pan de-soñs

Can you give me a can of – Est-ce que vous pouvez me donner un
petrol please? bidon d'essence s'il vous plaît?
es-kuh voo poo-vay muh do-nay uñ bee-doñ de-soñs see voo play?

There is something wrong – Il y a quelque chose qui ne va pas dans
with my car ma voiture
eel ya kel-kuh-shōz kee nuh va pa doñ ma vwah-tōōr

Can you find the trouble? – Est-ce que vous pouvez trouver ce qui ne
va pas?
es-kuh voo poo-vay troo-vay suh kee nuh va pa?

I have a flat tyre – J'ai crevé
zhay kruh-vay

The battery is dead – La batterie est à plat
la ba-tree et a pla

My windscreen (windshield) – Mon pare-brise est cassé
has shattered *moñ par-breez ay ka-say*

The engine's overheating – Le moteur chauffe
luh mō-tur shōf

Driving
Breakdowns & Repairs

There is a leak in the radiator – Il y a une fuite dans le radiateur
eel ee a ōōn fweet doñ luh rad-ya-tur

I have blown a fuse – C'est un fusible qui est grillé
set uñ fōō-zee-bluh kee ay gree-yay

The exhaust pipe has fallen off – Le pot d'échappement est tombé
luh pō day-shap-moñ ay toñ-bay

There is a bad connection – Il y a un mauvais contact
eel ee a uñ mō-ve koñ-takt

I have lost the ignition key – J'ai perdu la clé de contact
zhay per-dōō la klay duh koñ-takt

I need a new fan belt – J'ai besoin d'une nouvelle courroie de ventilateur
zhay buh-zwañ dōōn noo-vel koor-wah duh voñ-tee-la-tur

Can you replace the windscreen wiper blades? – Est-ce que vous pouvez remplacer mes balais d'essuie-glace?
es-kuh voo poo-vay roñ-pla-say may ba-lay des-wee-glas?

Is it serious? – Est-ce que c'est grave?
es-kuh say grahv?

How long will it take to repair it? – La réparation prendra combien de temps?
la ray-pa-ras-yoñ proñ-dra koñ-byeñ duh toñ?

Do you have the parts? – Est-ce que vous avez les pièces de rechange?
es-kuh voo za-vay lay pyes duh ruh-shoñzh?

Can you fix it for the time being? – Est-ce que vous pouvez le réparer provisoirement?
es-kuh voo poo-vay luh ray-pa-ray pro-veez-war-moñ?

Can I have an itemized bill for my insurance company? – Est-ce que je peux avoir une facture détaillée pour ma compagnie d'assurance?
es-kuh zhuh puh zav-war ōōn fak-tōōr day-tye-yay poor ma koñ-pan-yee da-sōō-roñs?

Driving The Car

accelerator	l'accélérateur *lax-ay-lay-ra-tur*	distributor	le delco *luh del-kō*
air filter	le filtre à air *luh feel-tra-er*	door	la portière *la port-yer*
alternator	l'alternateur *lal-ter-na-tur*	dynamo	la dynamo *là dee-na-mō*
automatic transmission	la transmission automatique *la troñz-mees-yoñ ō-tō-ma-teek*	electrical system	le système électrique *luh see-stem ay-lek-treek*
axle	l'essieu *les-yuh*	engine	le moteur *luh mō-tur*
backup light	le phare de recul *luh far duh ruh-kōol*	exhaust system	l'échappement *lay-shap-moñ*
battery	la batterie *la ba-tree*	fan belt	la courroie de ventilateur *la koor-wah duh voñ-tee-la-tur*
bonnet	le capot *luh ka-pō*	fuel gauge	la jauge d'essence *la zhōzh de-soñs*
boot	le coffre *luh kof-ruh*	fuel pump	la pompe à essence *la poñp a e-soñs*
brakes	les freins *lay frañ*	fuse	le fusible *luh fōo-zee-bluh*
brake fluid	le liquide de frein *luh lee-keed duh frañ*	gear box	la boîte de vitesses *la bwaht duh vee-tes*
carburettor	le carburateur *luh kar-bōo-ra-tur*	gear lever (shift)	le levier de vitesses *luh luh-vyay duh vee-tes*
choke	le starter *luh star-ter*		
clutch	l'embrayage *loñ-bray-yazh*	generator	la dynamo *la dee-na-mō*
cooling system	le système de refroidissement *luh see-stem duh ruh-frwah-dees-moñ*	handbrake	le frein à main *luh frañ a mañ*
		headlights	les phares *lay far*
cylinder	le cylindre *luh see-lañ-druh*	heating system	le chauffage *luh shō-fazh*
disc brake	le frein à disque *luh frañ a deesk*		

Driving
The Car

hood	le capot *luh ka-pō*	**shock** **absorber**	l'amortisseur *la-mor-tee-sur*
horn	le klaxon *luh klak-soñ*	**silencer**	le silencieux *luh see-loñs-yuh*
hose	la durite *la dōō-reet*	**spanner**	la clé *la klay*
ignition	l'allumage *la-lōō-mazh*	**spare**	la pièce de rechange *la pyes duh ruh-shoñzh*
ignition key	la clé de contact *la klay duh koñ-takt*	**spark plug**	la bougie *la boo-zhee*
indicator	le clignotant *luh kleen-yo-toñ*	**starter motor**	le démarreur *luh day-ma-rur*
jack	le cric *luh kreek*	**steering**	la direction *la dee-rex-yoñ*
lights	les feux *lay fuh*	**stoplight**	le voyant *luh vwah-yoñ*
muffler	le silencieux *luh see-loñs-yuh*	**suspension**	la suspension *la sōō-spoñs-yoñ*
oil	l'huile *lweel*	**transmission**	la transmission *la troñs-mees-yoñ*
oil filter	le filtre à huile *luh feel-tra weel*	**trunk**	le coffre *luh kof-ruh*
oil pressure **gauge**	le manomètre d'huile *luh ma-nō-met-ruh* *dweel*	**turn** **indicator**	le clignotant *luh kleen-yo-toñ*
petrol	l'essence *le-soñs*	**tyre**	le pneu *luh pnuh*
radiator	le radiateur *luh rad-ya-tur*	**tyre pressure**	la pression des pneus *la pres-yoñ day pnuh*
rear-view **mirror**	le rétroviseur *luh ray-trō-vee-zur*	**warning light**	le voyant *luh vwah-yoñ*
reversing **light**	le phare de recul *luh far duh ruh-kōōl*	**water**	l'eau *lō*
seat	le siège *luh syezh*	**wheel**	la roue *la roo*
seat belt	la ceinture de sécurité *la señ-tōōr duh* *say-kōō-ree-tay*	**windscreen/** **windshield**	le pare-brise *luh par-breez*
		wipers	les essuie-glace *lay-zes-wee-glas*
		wrench	la clé *la klay*

Driving
Accidents & the Police

I'm very sorry officer	Je suis désolé, Monsieur *zhuh swee day-zo-lay muh-syuh*
I did not see the signal	Je n'ai pas vu le panneau *zhuh nay pa vōō luh pa-nō*
I did not know about that regulation	Je ne connaissais pas ce règlement *zhuh nuh ko-ne-se pa suh reg-luh-moñ*
I did not understand the sign	Je n'ai pas compris le panneau *zhuh nay pa koñ-pree luh pa-nō*
Here is my driving licence	Voilà mon permis *vwah-la moñ per-mee*
Here is my green card	Voilà ma carte verte *vwah-la ma kart vert*
How much is the fine?	La contravention est de combien? *la koñ-tra-voñs-yoñ ay duh koñ-byeñ?*
I haven't got that much. Can I pay at the police station?	Je n'ai pas assez. Est-ce que je peux payer au poste de police? *zhuh nay pa zas-ay. es-kuh zhuh puh pay-ay ō post duh po-lees?*
I was driving at 80 Kmh	Je roulais à quatre-vingts kilomètres à l'heure *zhuh roo-le za kat-ruh-vañ kee-lō-met-ra lur*
He was too close	Il me suivait de trop près *eel me swee-ve duh trō pre*
I did not see him	Je ne l'ai pas vu *zhuh nuh lay pa vōō*
He was driving too fast	Il conduisait trop vite *eel koñ-dwee-ze trō veet*
He did not stop	Il ne s'est pas arrêté *eel nuh say pa za-re-tay*
He did not give way (yield)	Il n'a pas respecté la priorité *eel na pa res-pek-tay la pree-o-ree-tay*
He stopped very suddenly	Il s'est arrêté brusquement *eel set a-re-tay brōōsk-moñ*

Driving
Accidents & the Police

He swerved – Il a donné un coup de volant
eel a do-nay uñ koo duh vo-loñ

The car turned without signalling – La voiture a tourné sans clignoter
ta vwah-tōōr a toor-nay soñ kleen-yō-tay

He ran into me – Il m'est rentré dedans
eel may roñ-tray duh-doñ

He overtook on a bend (passed on a curve) – Il m'a dépassé dans le virage
eel ma day-pa-say doñ luh vee-razh

His car number (license number) was . . . – Le numéro de la voîture était . . .
luh nōō-may-rō duh la vwah-tōōr ay-té .

The road was wet – La route était mouillée
la root ay-te moo-yay

I skidded – J'ai dérapé
zhay day-ra-pay

My brakes failed – Mes freins ont lâché
may frañ oñ la-shay

I had a blow-out – Un pneu a éclaté
uñ pnuh a ay-kla-tay

I could not stop in time – Je n'ai pas pu m'arrêter à temps
zhuh nay pa pōō ma-re-tay a toñ

What is your name and address? – Quel est votre nom et votre adresse?
kel ay vo-truh noñ ay vot-ra-dres?

We should call the police – Nous devrions appeler la police
noo duh-vree-yoñ zap-lay la po-lees

Hotels

Hotels are officially grouped into categories of 1, 2, 3 or 4 stars and further graded as A, B or C. You can also stay at one of the *relais routiers* (primarily for lorry-drivers, but of a good standard) or, in country areas, in a *logis de France*. Many hotels can handle a booking in English, but if you don't want to take any chances . . .

Dear Sir,
Monsieur,

I wish to stay in Tours from 5/6/85 to 9/6/85
Je souhaite séjourner à Tours du 5/6/85 au 9/6/85

– **with my wife**
avec ma femme

– **with my family**
avec ma famille

Can you provide the following accommodation
Est-ce que vous auriez

– **1 single room with shower**
1 chambre pour une personne avec douche

– **1 twin-bedded room with bath**
1 chambre avec lits jumeaux et salle de bain

– **1 double room (with a bed for a child)**
1 chambre pour deux personnes (avec un lit pour un enfant)

Please inform me of your inclusive rates for
Je vous prie de me communiquer vos prix T.T.C. pour

– **room and breakfast**
la chambre avec petit déjeuner

– **room and evening meal**
la demi-pension

– **room and all meals**
la pension complète

I enclose an International Reply coupon
Veuillez trouver ci-joint un coupon-réponse international

Yours faithfully,
Recevez, Monsieur, l'expression de mes sentiments distingués,

You'll have to cope with the reply yourself, but if everything is all right it will mention prices; if it begins *'nous avons le regret'*, you may have problems. If you're checking in on the spot. . .

My name is . . . — Je m'appelle . . .
zhuh ma-pel . . .

I reserved a room — J'ai réservé une chambre
zhay ray-zer-vay ōōn shoñ-bruh

Do you have a single room? — Avez-vous une chambre pour une personne?
a-vay voo zōōn shoñ-bruh poor ōōn per-son?

Do you have a room with twin beds and shower? — Avez-vous une chambre avec lits jumeaux et douche?
a-vay voo zōōn shoñ-bruh a-vek lee zhōō-mō ay doosh?

Do you have a double room with bath? — Avez-vous une chambre pour deux personnes avec salle de bains?
a-vay voo zōōn shoñ-bruh poor duh per-son a-vek sal duh bañ?

I want to stay for 3 nights — Je désire rester trois nuits
zhuh day-zeer res-tay trwah nwee

We shall be staying until the sixth of May — Nous resteroñs jusqu'au six mai
noo res-troñ zhōō-skō see me

How much is the room per night? — La chambre fait combien pour une nuit?
la shoñ-bruh fe koñ-byeñ poor ōōn nwee?

Is that inclusive? — Toutes taxes comprises?
toot tax koñ-preez?

How much is the room and evening meal? — La demi-pension fait combien?
la duh-mee poñ-syoñ fe koñ-byeñ?

How much is the room and all meals? — La pension complète fait combien?
la poñ-syoñ koñ-plet fe koñ-byeñ?

Have you got a cot (crib) for our baby? — Est-ce que vous avez un berceau pour notre bébé?
es-kuh voo za-vay zuñ ber-sō poor not-ruh bay-bay?

Hotels

What time is À quelle heure est *a kel ur ay*	– **breakfast?** le petit déjeuner? *luh puh-tee day-zhuh-nay?*
	– **lunch?** le déjeuner? *luh day-zhuh-nay?*
	– **dinner?** le dîner? *luh dee-nay?*
Can we have breakfast in our room please?	– Est-ce que nous pourrions avoir le petit déjeuner dans notre chambre, s'il vous plaît? *es-kuh noo poo-ree-yoñ za-vwar luh puh-tee day-zhuh-nay doñ no-truh shoñ-bruh see voo play?*
Where can I park the car?	– Où est-ce que je peux garer la voiture? *oo es-kuh zhuh puh ga-ray la vwah-tōōr?*
What time does the hotel close?	– L'hôtel ferme à quelle heure? *lō-tel ferm a kel ur?*
Is there a lift (elevator)?	– Est-ce qu'il y a un ascenseur? *es-keel ya uñ na-soñ-sur?*
Can I drink the tap-water?	– Est-ce que l'eau du robinet est potable? *es-kuh lō dōō ro-bee-nay ay po-tab-luh?*
Please call me at 8 o'clock	– Réveillez-moi à huit heures s'il vous plaît *ray-vay-yay mwah a weet ur see voo play*
Can I leave these for safe-keeping?	– Est-ce que je peux déposer ces affaires dans votre coffre? *es-kuh zhuh puh day-pō-zay say za-fer doñ vot-ruh kof-ruh?*
Can I have my things back from the safe?	– Est-ce que je peux récupérer les affaires que j'ai déposées dans votre coffre? *es-kuh zhuh puh ray-kōō-pay-ray lay za-fer kuh zhay day-pō-zay doñ vot-ruh kof-ruh?*
Can I make a telephone call from here?	– Est-ce que je peux téléphoner d'ici? *es-kuh zhuh puh tay-lay-fō-nay dee-see?*

Is the voltage 220 or 110?	– Est-ce que le voltage est du 220 ou du 110? *es-kuh luh vol-tazh ay dōō duh soñ vañ oo dōō soñ dees?*
Can I have Est-ce que je peux avoir *es-kuh zhuh puh za-vwar*	– **my key?** ma clef? *ma klay?*
	– **some coat hangers?** des portemanteaux? *day port-moñ-tō?*
	– **some notepaper?** du papier à lettres? *dōō pap-yay a let-ruh?*
	– **an ashtray?** un cendrier? *uñ soñd-ree-ay?*
	– **another blanket?** une autre couverture? *ōōn ō-truh koo-ver-tōōr?*
	– **another pillow?** un autre orciller? *uñ nō-truh o-ray-yay?*
Where is the socket (outlet) for my razor?	– Où est la prise pour mon rasoir? *oo ay la preez poor moñ ra-zwar?*
There are no towels in the room	– Il n'y a pas de serviettes dans la chambre *eel nee ya pa duh serv-yet doñ la shoñ-bruh*
The room is too noisy	– La chambre est trop bruyante *la shoñ-bruh ay trō brwee-yoñt*
I cannot open the window	– Je ne peux pas ouvrir la fenêtre *zhuh nuh puh pa zoo-vreer la fnet-ruh*
The light is not working	– La lumière ne marche pas *la lōōm-yer nuh marsh pa*
The air-conditioning is not working	– L'air conditionné ne marche pas *ler koñ-dees-yo-nay nuh marsh pa*

Hotels

The heating is not working – Le chauffage ne marche pas
luh shō-fazh nuh marsh pa

I cannot turn the heating off – Je ne peux pas éteindre le chauffage
zhuh nuh puh pa zay-tañ-druh luh shō-fazh

The lock is broken – La serrure est cassée
la se-rōōr ay ka-say

There is no hot water – Il n'y a pas d'eau chaude
eel nee ya pa dō shōd

The washbasin is dirty – Le lavabo est sale
luh la-va-bō ay sal

The plug is broken – La bonde est cassée
la boñd ay ka-say

There is no toilet paper – Il n'y a pas de papier hygiénique
eel nee ya pa duh pap-yay ee-zhay-neek

Do you have a laundry room? – Est-ce que vous avez une lingerie?
es-kuh voo za-vay zōōn lañzh-ree?

I want to iron some clothes – Je voudrais repasser des affaires
zhuh voo-dre ruh-pa-say day za-fer

I want to stay an extra night – Je voudrais rester une nuit
supplémentaire
zhuh voo-dre res-tay ōōn nwee sōō-play-moñ-ter

We will be leaving at 9 o'clock tomorrow morning – Nous partirons demain matin à neuf
heures
noo par-tee-roñ duh-mañ ma-tañ a nuh vur

I would like the bill please – La note, s'il vous plaît
la not see voo play

Do you accept traveller's cheques? – Est-ce que vous acceptez les chèques de
voyage?
es-kuh voo zax-ep-tay lay shek duh vwah-yazh?

Could you have my luggage brought down? – Est-ce que vous pourriez faire descendre
mes bagages?
es-kuh voo poo-ree-ay fer de-soñ-druh may ba-gazh?

Can you order me a taxi?	– Est-ce que vous pourriez m'appeler un taxi?
	es-kuh voo poo-ree-ay ma-play uñ tax-ee?
Thank you. We enjoyed our stay	– Merci. Nous avons passé un agréable séjour
	mer-see. noo za-voñ pa-say uñ na-gray-ab-luh say-zhoor

If you're a typical absent-minded visitor, you might need this type of letter:

Dear Sir,

I recently spent some time in your hotel in room 16. I believe I forgot

> **a pair of shoes**

when I left. If you would be good enough to send them on to me I would be most grateful and refund the cost of postage.

> **Yours faithfully,**

Cher Monsieur,

Je suis récemment descendu dans votre hôtel – chambre 16. Je pense avoir oublié

> une paire de chaussures

en partant. Auriez-vous l'amabilité de me les envoyer. Je vous en serais très reconnaissant et vous rembourserais les frais de poste dès réception. Je vous prie de croire, cher Monsieur, à l'expression de mes sentiments distingués,

Rented Villas

We have arranged to rent a house through your agency	– Nous avons loué une maison par votre agence *noo za-voñ loo-ay ōōn may-zoñ par vot ra-zhoñs*
Here is our booking	– Voici notre réservation *vwah-see not-ruh ray-zer-vas-yoñ*
We need two sets of.keys	– Nous avons besoin de deux jeux de clés *noo za-voñ buh-zwañ duh dih zhuh duh klay*
Will you show us round?	– Est-ce que vous pouvez nous faire visiter la maison? *es-kuh voo poo-vay noo fer vee-zee-tay la may-zoñ?*
Which is the key for this door?	– Quelle clé ouvre cette porte? *kel klay oo-vruh set port?*
Where are the mains?	– Où est le compteur? *oo ay luh koñ-tur?*
Where is the water heater?	– Où est le chauffe-eau? *oo ay luh shō-fō?*
Please show me how this works	– Montrez-moi comment ça marche, s'il vous plaît *moñ-tray mwah ko-moñ sa marsh see voo play*
How does the heating work?	– Comment marche le chauffage? *ko-moñ marsh luh shō-fazh?*
When does the help come?	– La femme de ménage vient quand? *la fam duh may-nazh vyeñ koñ?*
Is there any spare bedding?	– Est-ce qu'il y a de la literie en supplément? *es-keel ya duh la leet-ree oñ sōō-play-moñ?*
Can I contact you if there are any problems?	– Est-ce que je peux vous contacter s'il y a des problèmes? *es-kuh zhuh puh voo koñ-tak-tay seel ya day prob-lem?*
The cooker (stove) does not work	– La cuisinière ne marche pas *la kwee-zeen-yer nuh marsh pa*

I can't open the windows – Je ne peux pas ouvrir les fenêtres
zhuh nuh puh pa zoo-vreer lay fnet-ruh

We can't get any water – Nous n'avons pas d'eau
noo na-voñ pa dō

The toilet won't flush – La chasse d'eau ne marche pas
la shas dō nuh marsh pa

A fuse has blown – Un plomb a sauté
uñ ploñ a sō-tay

There is a gas leak – Il y a une fuite de gaz
eel ee a ōōn fweet duh gaz

I need somebody to fix this – J'ai besoin de quelqu'un pour réparer ça
zhay buh-zwañ duh kel-kuñ poor ray-pa-ray sa

bath	la baignoire *la beny-war*	**knife**	le couteau *luh koo-tō*
bathroom	la salle de bain *la sal duh bañ*	**pan**	la casserole *la kas-rol*
bed	le lit *luh lee*	**plate**	l'assiette *las-yet*
blanket	la couverture *la koo-ver-tōōr*	**refrigerator**	le frigidaire *luh free-zhee-der*
brush	la brosse *la bros*	**sheet**	le drap *luh dra*
can opener	l'ouvre-boîte *loo-vruh-bwaht*	**sink**	l'évier *lay-vyay*
chair	la chaise *la shez*	**spoon**	la cuillère *la kwee-yer*
cooker	la cuisinière *la kwee-zeen-yer*	**table**	la table *la tab-luh*
corkscrew	le tire-bouchon *luh teer-boo-shoñ*	**tap**	le robinet *luh ro-bee-nay*
fork	la fourchette *la foor-shet*	**toilet**	les toilettes *lay twah-let*
frying pan	la poêle *la pwahl*	**vacuum cleaner**	l'aspirateur *las-pee-ra-tur*
kitchen	la cuisine *la kwee-zeen*	**washbasin**	le lavabo *luh la-va-bō*

Travelling with a Family

If you take the kids – *les gosses* – away with you, anything can happen and probably will, but these phrases should be useful in at least some of the situations you'll encounter.

There are four of us – Nous sommes quatre
noo som kat-ruh

my wife – ma femme
ma fam

my husband – mon mari
moñ ma-ree

my daughter – ma fille
ma fee

my son – mon fils
moñ fees

Have you got a cot (crib) for our baby? – Est-ce que vous avez un berceau pour notre bébé?
es-kuh voo za-vay zuñ ber-sō poor not-ruh bay-bay?

Can my son sleep in our room? – Est-ce que mon fils peut dormir dans notre chambre?
es-kuh moñ fees puh dor-meer doñ not-ruh shoñ-bruh?

Are there any other children in the hotel? – Est-ce qu'il y a d'autres enfants dans l'hôtel?
es-keel ya dō-truh zoñ-foñ doñ lō-tel?

How old are your children? – Quel âge ont vos enfants?
kel azh oñ vō zoñ-foñ?

The boy is 9 years old – Le garçon a neuf ans
luh gar-soñ a nuh voñ

The girl is 15 months – La fille a quinze mois
la fee a kañz mwah

Where can I feed my baby? – Où est-ce que je peux allaiter mon bébé?
oo es-kuh zhuh puh za-lay-tay moñ bay-bay?

I need some disposable nappies (diapers) – J'ai besoin de couches à jeter
zhay buh-zwañ duh koosh a zhuh-tay

Travelling with a Family

Can you warm this bottle for me?	– Voulez-vous me réchauffer ce biberon? *voo-lay voo muh ray-shō-fay suh beeb-roñ?*
Have you got a high chair?	– Est-ce que vous avez une chaise de bébé? *es-kuh voo za-vay zōōn shez duh bay-bay?*
Do you know anyone who will babysit for us?	– Est-ce que vous connaissez quelqu'un qui pourrait garder nos enfants? *es-kuh voo ko-ne-say kel-kuñ kee poo-re gar-day nō zoñ-foñ?*
We will be back at 11	– Nous rentrons à onze heures *noo roñ-troñ a oñz ur*
She goes to bed at 8	– Elle se couche à huit heures *el suh koosh a weet ur*
Are there any organized activities for the children?	– Est-ce qu'il y a des activités organisées pour les enfants? *es-keel ya day zak-tee-vee-tay or-ga-nee-zay poor lay zoñ-foñ?*
Is there a paddling pool?	– Est-ce qu'il y a un petit bassin pour les enfants? *es-keel ya uñ puh-tee ba-sañ poor lay zoñ-foñ?*
Is there an amusement park?	– Est-ce qu'il y a un parc d'attractions? *es-keel ya uñ par da-trax-yoñ?*
Is there a zoo nearby?	– Est-ce qu'il y a un zoo dans les environs? *es-keel ya uñ zō doñ lay zoñ-vee-roñ?*
My son has hurt himself	– Mon fils s'est blessé *moñ fees say ble-say*
My daughter is ill	– Ma fille est malade *ma fee ay ma-lad*
I'm very sorry – he shouldn't have done that	– Pardon, madame (*etc*), il n'aurait pas dû faire ça *par-doñ ma-dam, eel nō-re pa dōō fer sa*

Camping

Camping in France is a very sophisticated activity, with campers bringing lots of home comforts with them. There are a great number of official camping sites, many with excellent facilities. It helps if you have an International Camping Carnet. If you can't find a site, the local *syndicat d'initiative* may be able to help.

Is there anywhere for us to camp near here?	– Est-ce que nous pouvons camper quelque part dans les environs? *es-kuh noo poo-voñ koñ-pay kel-kuh par doñ lay zoñ-vee-roñ?*
Have you got a site for our tent?	– Est-ce qu'il y a un emplacement pour notre tente? *es-keel ya uñ noñ-plas-moñ poor not-ruh toñt?*
Do you mind if we camp on your land?	– Est-ce que nous pouvons camper sur votre terrain, s'il vous plaît? *es-kuh noo poo-voñ koñ-pay sōōr vot-ruh te-rañ see voo play?*
This site is very muddy	– Ce terrain est très boueux *suh te-rañ ay tray boo-uh*
Could we have a more sheltered site?	Est-ce que nous pourrions avoir un endroit plus abrité? *es-kuh noo poo-ree-yoñ za-vwar uñ noñ-drwah plōō za-bree-tay?*
Can we put our caravan (trailer) here?	– Est-ce que nous pouvons mettre notre caravane ici? *es-kuh noo poo-voñ me-truh not-ruh ka-ra-van ee-see?*
Is there a shop on the site?	– Est-ce qu'il y a un magasin dans le camp? *es-keel ya uñ ma-ga-zañ doñ luh koñ?*
Can I have a shower?	– Est-ce que je peux prendre une douche? *es-kuh zhuh puh proñ-druh ōōn doosh?*
Where is the drinking water?	– Où est l'eau potable? *oo ay lō pō-ta-bluh?*
Where are the toilets and washroom?	– Où sont les toilettes et les lavabos? *oo soñ lay twah-let ay lay la-va-bō?*

Camping Equipment

Where can we wash our dishes? – Où peut-on faire la vaisselle?
oo puh-toñ fer la ve-sel?

Is there another camp-site near here? – Est-ce qu'il y a un autre camping près d'ici?
es-keel ya uñ nō-truh koñ-peeng pre dee-see?

air-mattress	le matelas pneumatique *luh mat-la pnuh-ma-teek*	**ground**	le sol *luh sol*
back pack	le sac à dos *luh sak a dō*	**guy line**	la ficelle *la fee-sel*
bottle opener	l'ouvre-bouteille *loo-vruh-boo-tay*	**knife**	le couteau *luh koo-tō*
bucket	le seau *luh sō*	**mallet**	le maillet *luh mye-yay*
camp bed	le lit de camp *luh lee duh koñ*	**matches**	les allumettes *lay za-lōō-met*
camp chair	la chaise de camping *la shez duh koñ-peeng*	**pail**	le seau *luh sō*
candle	la bougie *la boo-zhee*	**penknife**	le canif *luh ka-neef*
can opener	l'ouvre-boîte *loo-vruh-bwaht*	**plate**	l'assiette *las-yet*
cup	la tasse *la tas*	**rucksack**	le sac à dos *luh sak a dō*
fire	le feu *luh fuh*	**shelter**	l'abri *la-bree*
flashlight	la lampe électrique *la loñp ay-lek-treek*	**sleeping bag**	le sac de couchage *luh sak duh koo-shazh*
fly sheet	le double toit *luh doo-bluh twah*	**stove**	le réchaud *luh ray-shō*
folding table	la table pliante *la tah-bluh plee-yoñt*	**tent peg**	le piquet de tente *luh pee-kay duh toñt*
fork	la fourchette *la foor-shet*	**tent pole**	le mât de tente *luh mah duh toñt*
frying pan	la poêle *la pwahl*	**thermos flask**	la bouteille thermos *la boo-tay ter-mos*
		torch	la lampe électrique *la loñp ay-lek-treek*

Youth Hostels

Here is my youth hostel card	– Voici ma carte d'auberge de jeunesse *vwah-see ma kart dō-berzh duh zhuh-nes*
How long can I stay?	– Je peux rester combien de nuits? *zhuh puh res-tay koñ-byeñ duh nwee?*
I want to stay two nights here	– Je désire rester deux nuits ici *zhuh day-zeer res-tay duh nwee ee-see*
I would like to join here	– Je voudrais acheter la carte de membre ici *zhuh voo-dre zash-tay la kart duh moñ-bree-see*
Are you open during the day?	– Est-ce que vous êtes ouverts pendant la journée? *es-kuh voo zet zoo-ver poñ-doñ la zhoor-nay?*
What time do you close?	– Vous fermez à quelle heure? *voo fer-may a kel ur?*
Do you serve meals?	– Est-ce que vous servez des repas? *es-kuh voo ser-vay day ruh-pa?*
Can I use the kitchen?	– Est-ce que je peux utiliser la cuisine? *es-kuh zhuh puh zōō-tee-lee-zay la kwee-zeen?*
I want to rent a sheet sleeping bag	– Je désire louer un sac à viande *zhuh day-zeer loo-ay uñ sak a vyoñd*
Is there another youth hostel near here?	– Est-ce qu'il y a une autre auberge de jeunesse dans les environs? *es-keel ya ōōn ō-trō-berzh duh zhuh-nes doñ lay zoñ-vee-roñ?*

Where is there – **a Catholic church?**
Où y a-t-il   une église catholique?
oo ee a-teel   *ōōn ay-gleez ka-to-leek?*

– **a Protestant church?**
un temple?
uñ toñ-pluh?

– **a Baptist church?**
un temple baptiste?
uñ toñ-pluh ba-teest?

– **a synagogue?**
une synagogue?
ōōn see-na-gog?

– **a mosque?**
une mosquée?
ōōn mos-kay?

What time is the service? – L'office est à quelle heure?
lo-fees et a kel ur?

I'd like to see – **a priest . . .**
Je voudrais voir   un prêtre
zhuh voo-dre vwar   *uñ pret-ruh*

– **a minister . . .**
un pasteur
uñ pas-tur

– **a rabbi . . .**
un rabin
uñ ra-bañ

. . . who speaks English – qui parle anglais
kee parl oñ-glay

The Weather

You may need to know the weather forecast, or you may just want to make conversation . . .

It's a lovely day	– Il fait beau *eel fay bō*
It's too hot for me	– Il fait trop chaud pour moi *eel fay trō shō poor mwah*
There's a nice breeze	– Il y a un petit vent agréable *eel ya uñ puh-tee voñ tag-ray-ah-bluh*
It's raining	– Il pleut *eel pluh*
It's windy	– Il fait du vent *eel fay dōo voñ*
It's snowing	– Il neige *eel nezh*
It's foggy	– Il fait du brouillard *eel fay dōo broo-yar*
It's cold	– Il fait froid *eel fay frwah*
Is it going Est-ce qu'il va *es-keel va*	– **to be fine?** faire beau? *fer bō?*
	– **to rain?** pleuvoir? *pluh-vwar?*
	– **to be windy?** faire du vent? *fer dōo voñ?*
	– **to snow?** neiger? *ne-zhay?*
What is the temperature?	– Il fait combien? *eel fay koñ-byeñ?*
Is the weather going to change?	– Est-ce que le temps va changer? *es-kuh luh toñ va shoñ-zhay?*

The Weather

Will the weather improve? – Est-ce qu'il va faire meilleur?
es-keel va fer may-yur?

Is it going to get cooler? – Est-ce qu'il va faire plus frais?
es-keel va fer ploo fray?

Will the wind go down? – Est-ce que le vent va tomber?
es-kuh luh voñ va toñ-bay?

Is there going to be a thunderstorm? – Est-ce qu'il va y avoir un orage?
es-keel va ee a-vwar uñ nō-razh?

Is the sea calm? – Est-ce que la mer est calme?
es-kuh la mer ay kalm?

Is the water warm? – Est-ce que l'eau est chaude?
es-kuh lō ay shōd?

When is high tide? – La marée haute est à quelle heure?
la ma-ray ōt et a kel ur?

It's a clear night – La nuit est claire
la nwee ay kler

Will it be cold tonight? – Est-ce qu'il fera froid ce soir?
es-keel fra frwah suh swar?

The stars are out – Le ciel est plein d'étoiles
luh syel ay plañ day-twahl

Leisure & Entertainment
On the Beach

The flags to look out for on French beaches are not red, white and blue, but red, green or orange. If you see a red flag – don't go swimming, it's not safe and there's no lifeguard. If the flag's orange, it's still unsafe, but there is a lifeguard around. The green flag means that you can go right ahead!

Is it safe to swim here?	– Est-ce qu'il est prudent de nager ici?
	es-keel ay prōō-doñ duh na-zhay ee-see?
Is this a private beach?	– Est-ce une plage privée, ici?
	es ōōn plahzh pree-vay ee-see?
Can you recommend a quiet beach?	– Est-ce que vous connaissez une plage tranquille?
	es-kuh voo ko-nay-say ōōn plahzh troñ-keel?
Where can we change?	– Où sont les vestiaires?
	oo soñ lay vest-yer?

Can I rent	**– a deck chair?**
Est-ce que je peux louer	un transat?
es-kuh zhuh puh loo-ay	*uñ troñ-zat?*
	– a sunshade?
	un parasol?
	uñ pa-ra-sol?
	– a sailing boat?
	un voilier?
	uñ vwahl-yay?

Is it possible to go	**– sailing?**
Est-ce qu'il est possible de faire	de la voile?
es-keel ay po-see-bluh duh fer	*duh la vwahl?*
	– water-skiing?
	du ski nautique?
	dōō skee nō-teek?
	– surfing?
	du surf?
	dōō sōōrf?
	– wind surfing?
	de la planche à voile?
	duh la ploñsh a vwahl?

Leisure & Entertainment
Outdoors & Nightlife

Is there a swimming pool? – Est-ce qu'il y a une piscine?
es-keel ya ōōn pee-seen?

Is there somewhere I can play – **tennis?**
Est-ce que je peux jouer   au tennis quelque part?
es-kuh zhuh puh zhoo-ay   *ō te-nees kel-kuh par?*

                     – **golf?**
                     au golf quelque part?
                     ō golf kel-kuh par?

Is it possible to go riding? – Est-ce qu'il est possible de faire du cheval?
es-keel ay po-see-bluh duh fer dōō shuh-val?

Can I go fishing? – Est-ce que je peux aller à la pêche?
es-kuh zhuh puh za-lay a la pesh?

Can I rent the equipment? – Est-ce que je peux louer le matériel?
es-kuh zhuh puh loo-ay luh ma-tay-ree-el?

Do you know any interesting – Est-ce que vous connaissez des
walks? promenades intéressantes à faire?
es-kuh voo ko-nay-say day prom-nad añ-tay-re-soñt à fer?

Are there any local festivals – Est-ce qu'il y a des fêtes locales près
nearby? d'ici?
es-keel ya day fet lō-kal pre dee-see?

Are there any films in – Est-ce qu'il y a des films en anglais?
English? *es-keel ya day feelm oñ noñ-glay?*

Is there a concert? – Est-ce qu'il y a un concert?
es-keel ya uñ koñ-ser?

2 balcony tickets, please – Deux balcons s'il vous plaît
duh bal-koñ seè voo play

2 stalls (orchestra) tickets, – Deux orchestres s'il vous plaît
please *duh zor-kest-ruh see voo play*

Are there any good night – Est-ce qu'il y a de bonnes boîtes de nuit?
clubs? *es-keel ya duh bon bwaht duh nwee?*

Is there a disco? – Est-ce qu'il y a une discothèque?
es keel ya ōōn dee-skō-tek?

Sightseeing

What is there to see here?	– Qu'est-ce qu'il y a à voir ici? *kes-keel ya a vwar ee-see?*
Have you got a town guide?	– Est-ce que vous avez une brochure sur la ville? *es-kuh voo za-vay zōōn bro-shōōr sōōr la veel?*
What is this building?	– Qu'est-ce que c'est, ce bâtiment? *kes-kuh say suh ba-tee-moñ?*
When was it built?	– Il a été construit à quelle date? *eel a ay-tay koñ-strwee a kel dat?*
Is it open to the public?	– Est-ce qu'il est ouvert au public? *es-keel et oo-ver tō pōō-bleek?*
Are there any sightseeing tours?	– Est-ce qu'il y a des visites guidées? *es-keel ya day vee-zeet gee-day?*
Is there a tour of the castle?	– Est-ce qu'il y a une visite guidée du château? *es-keel ya ōōn vee-zeet gee-day dōō sha-tō?*
When is thè bus tour of the town?	– À quelle heure est la visite guidée de la ville en autobus? *a kel ur ay la vee-zeet gee-day duh la veel oñ nō-tō-bōōs?*
How long does the tour take?	– Combien de temps dure la visite? *koñ-byeñ duh toñ dōōr la vee-zeet?*
Are there any boat trips on the river?	– Est-ce qu'il y a des voyages en bateau sur la rivière? *es-keel ya day vwah-yazh oñ ba-tō sōōr la ree-vyer?*
Are there any guided tours of the cathedral?	– Est-ce qu'il y a des visites guidées de la cathédrale? *es-keel yn day vee-zeet gee-day duh la ka-tay-dral?*
Is there an English-speaking guide?	– Est-ce qu'il y a un guide qui parle anglais? *es-keel ya uñ geed kee parl oñ-glay?*
What time does the museum open?	– À quelle heure ouvre le musée? *a kel ur oo-vruh luh mōō-zay?*

Have you got an English guidebook? – Est-ce que vous avez un guide en anglais?
es-kuh voo za-vay uñ geed oñ noñ-glay?

Can we go in? – Est-ce que nous pouvons entrer?
es-kuh noo poo-voñ zoñ-tray?

Are these monuments illuminated at night? – Est-ce que ces monuments sont éclairés la nuit?
es-kuh say mo-nōō-moñ soñ tay-klay-ray la nwee?

Is there a son et lumière display? – Est-ce qu'il y a un son et lumière?
es-keel ya uñ soñ ay lōōm-yer?

What is the admission charge? – C'est combien pour entrer?
say koñ-byeñ poor oñ-tray?

Can we go up to the top? – Est-ce que nous pouvons monter jusqu'en haut?
es-kuh noo poo-voñ moñ-tay zhōō-skoñ ō?

Where is the best view? – Où est la meilleure vue?
oo ay la may-yur vōō?

Can I take photos? – Est-ce que je peux prendre des photos?
es-kuh zhuh puh proñ-druh day phō-tō?

Can I use a flash? – Est-ce que je peux utiliser un flash?
es-kuh zhuh puh zōō-tee-lee-zay uñ flash?

Have you got any postcards? – Est-ce que vous avez des cartes postales?
es-kuh voo za-vay day kart po-stal?

Have you got any colour slides? – Est-ce que vous avez des diapos en couleur?
es-kuh voo za-vay day dee-ya-pō oñ koo-lur?

Where can you buy souvenirs? – Où peut-on acheter des souvenirs?
oo puh-toñ ash-tay day soov-neer?

Would you take a photo of us please? – Est-ce que vous voulez bien prendre une photo de nous s'il vous plaît?
es-kuh voo voo-lay byeñ proñ-druh ōōn phō-tō duh noo see voo play?

Eating & Drinking
Restaurants

A trip to France is an invitation to good eating; even if 4 star restaurants are out of your reach, the smaller ones are often memorable. Set price menus are often good value, but beware of *menus touristiques* in places obviously catering for tourists, where the standards are not likely to be high for customers who are only passing through. The best recommendation is the presence of the French themselves. The menu-reader on page 64 will help you decide what to eat: don't miss the opportunity to sample local specialities. Bon appétit!

Can we have a table for two? – Est-ce que nous pouvons avoir une table pour deux?
es-kuh noo poo-voñ za-vwar ōōn ta-bluh poor duh?

Can I reserve a table for four at 8 o'clock? – Est-ce que je peux réserver une table pour quatre à huit heures?
es-kuh zhuh puh ray-zer-vay ōōn ta-bluh poor kat-ruh a weet ur?

We'd like a table – **by the window**
Nous voudrions une table   près de la fenêtre
noo voo-dree-oñ zōōn ta-bluh   *pre duh la fnet-ruh*

– **on the terrace**
sur la terrasse
sōōr la te-ras

The menu, please – La carte s'il vous plaît
la kart see voo play

Have you got a set menu? – Est-ce que vous avez un menu?
es-kuh voo za-vay zuñ muh-nōō?

I will take the set menu – Je prendrai le menu
zhuh proñ-dray luh muh-nōō

We will take the menu at 35 francs – Nous prendrons le menu à trente-cinq francs
noo proñ-droñ luh muh-nōō a troñt-sañk froñ

Is this good? – Est-ce que c'est bon?
es-kuh say boñ?

Eating & Drinking
Restaurants

What is this dish like? – Ce plat est comment?
suh pla ay ko-moñ?

What do you recommend? – Qu'est-ce que vous me conseillez?
kes-kuh voo muh koñ-say-yay?

Have you got a local speciality? – Est-ce que vous avez une spécialité locale?
es-kuh voo za-vay zōōn spays-yal-ee-tay lō-kal?

I'll take that – Je prendrai cela
zhuh proñ-dray sla

We will begin with onion soup – Nous commencerons par une soupe à l'oignon
noo ko-moñs-roñ par ōōn soop a loñ-nyoñ

I will have steak and chips (French fries) – Je prendrai un steak-frites
zhuh proñ-dray uñ stayk-freet

I like it
Je le voudrais
zhuh luh voo-dre

– **very rare**
bleu
bluh

– **rare**
saignant
sen-yoñ

– **medium rare**
à point
a pwañ

– **well done**
bien cuit
byeñ kwee

Are vegetables included? – Est-ce que les légumes sont compris?
es-kuh lay lay-gōōm soñ koñ-pree?

Is this cheese very strong? – Est-ce que ce fromage est très fort?
es-kuh suh fro-mazh ay tray for?

That is not what I ordered – Ce n'est pas ce que j'ai commandé
snay pa suh kuh zhay ko-moñ-day

Eating & Drinking
Restaurants

That is for	**– me**
Ça, c'est pour	moi
sa, say poor	*mwah*
	– him
	Monsieur
	muhs-yuh
	– her
	Madame
	ma-dam
How do you eat this?	– On mange ça comment?
	oñ moñzh sa ko-moñ?
Could we have some more bread please?	– Du pain, s'il vous plaît
	dōō pañ see voo play
Could I have some butter?	– Du beurre, s'il vous plaît
	dōō bur see voo play
What is this called?	– Ça s'appelle comment?
	sa sa-pel ko-moñ?
Would you bring another glass please?	– Un autre verre s'il vous plaît
	uñ nō-truh ver see voo play
This is very salty	– Ceci est très salé
	suh-see ay tray sa-lay
I wanted cheese	– Je voulais du fromage
	zhuh voo-le dōō fro-mazh
Have you forgotten the soup?	– Est-ce que vous avez oublié la soupe?
	es-kuh voo za-vay zoo-blee-ay la soop?
This is cold	– Ceci est froid
	suh-see ay frwah
This is very good	– Ceci est très bon
	suh-see ay tray boñ
I'll have a dessert	– Je prendrai un dessert
	zhuh proñ-dray uñ de-ser

Eating & Drinking
Restaurants

The wine list please –	La carte des vins s'il vous plaît *la kart day vañ see voo play*
Which wine do you recommend? –	Quel vin me conseillez-vous? *kel vañ muh koñ-say-yay voo?*
Is the local wine good? –	Est-ce que le vin du pays est bon? *es-kuh luh vañ dōō pay-ee ay boñ?*
We'll take the Beaujolais –	Nous prendrons le Beaujolais *noo proñ-droñ luh bō-zho-le*
A small carafe (¼ litre) of red wine –	Un quart de rouge *uñ kar duh roozh*
A carafe (½ litre) of red wine –	Un demi de rouge *uñ duh-mee duh roozh*
A half bottle of white wine –	Une demi-bouteille de blanc *ōōn duh-mee boo-tay duh bloñ*
Another bottle please –	Une autre bouteille s'il vous plaît *ōōn ō-truh boo-tay see voo play*
Some plain water please –	Une carafe d'eau s'il vous plaît *ōōn ka-raf dō see voo play*
A bottle of mineral water –	Une bouteille d'eau minérale *ōōn boo-tay dō mee-nay-ral*
Black coffee, please –	Un café s'il vous plaît *uñ ka-fay see voo play*
Coffee with milk please –	Un café-crème s'il vous plaît *uñ ka-fay-krem see voo play*
The bill please –	L'addition s'il vous plaît *la-dees-yoñ see voo play*
Is service included? –	Est-ce que le service est compris? *es-kuh luh ser-vees ay koñ-pree?*
The meal was excellent –	Le repas était excellent *luh ruh-pa ay-tet ex-e-loñ*

Eating & Drinking
Menu Reader

Every area of France has its own specialities, and every self-respecting chef will create his own variations on traditional themes. In the list that follows we can only give some of the better-known dishes along with a few others that might make an interesting change if you happen to find them on the menu.

Andouille
Tripe sausage

Artichauts à la vinaigrette
Artichokes served with a bowl of vinaigrette sauce. You dip the fleshy part of the leaves in the sauce and eat it.

Asperges
Asparagus

Aubergines farcies
Stuffed aubergines (eggplants)

Bifteck
see Steak

Blanquette de veau
Stewed veal in a white sauce

Boeuf bourguignon
Beef stew with red wine

Boeuf en daube
Beef casserole

Boudin
Black (blood) pudding

Bouillabaisse
A speciality of Marseille, a soup/stew made with fish and shellfish

Caille sur canapé
Quail on toast

Canard à l'orange
Roast duck stuffed with orange and served with an orange and wine sauce

Canard rôti
Roast duck

Carottes Vichy
Slightly caramelized carrots cooked in sugar and butter

Cassoulet
A stew of beans with pork or mutton

Cervelles
Brains

Champignons à la crème
Mushrooms with cream sauce

Champignons à la grecque
Mushrooms served in oil, wine and herbs

Chipirons
Small octopus

Choucroûte garni
Sauerkraut garnished with assorted pork meats and boiled potatoes

Eating & Drinking
Menu Reader

Confit d'oie
Goose cooked and preserved in its own fat

Consommé
Clear soup

Coq au vin
Chicken cooked in red wine

Coquilles Saint-Jacques
Scallops served in their shells

Côtelettes de veau
Veal cutlets

Côtes de porc
Pork chops

Crudités
Assortment of raw vegetables (grated carrots, sliced tomatoes etc) served as an hors d'oeuvre

Dinde truffée
Truffled turkey

Entrecôte grillée
Grilled rib steak

Épaule d'agneau
Shoulder of lamb

Escalopes de veau à la crème
Veal escalopes in a cream sauce

Escargots à la bourguignonne
Snails in garlic butter sauce

Faisan rôti
Roast pheasant

Filet de sole meunière
Sole cooked in butter and served with lemon

Filets de sole normande
Sole in white wine with mushrooms, oysters and shrimps

Frites
Chips or French Fries

Gigot d'agneau rôti
Roast leg of lamb

Gratin dauphinois
Sliced potatoes with cheese and cream baked in the oven

Hachis parmentier
A sort of shepherd's pie – minced beef mixed in to mashed potatoes, then baked

Homard à l'armoricaine
Lobster sautéed with shallots, tomatoes, white wine; brandy is sometimes added

Huîtres
Oysters

Jambon de Bayonne
Raw, cured ham (from the Pays Basque)

Langouste
Crayfish

Langoustines
Scampi

Eating & Drinking
Menu Reader

Lapin chasseur
Rabbit cooked with white wine and herbs

Lapin de Garenne aux pruneaux
Wild rabbit marinated in a red wine and herb mixture, then casseroled with prunes

Lotte farcie
Stuffed turbot

Macédoine de légumes
Mixture of diced vegetables

Maquereaux au vin blanc
Mackerel in white wine

Morue Provençale
Cooked salt cod with tomatoes, onions, olives, capers, garlic and dressed in olive oil

Moules marinières
Mussels in white wine

Omelette
No translation needed, except for the filling:

aux champignons – mushrooms

aux fines herbes – mixed herbs

au fromage -- cheese

au jambon – ham

Paupiettes de veau
Thin rolls of veal with a forcemeat filling

Perdreau rôti
Roast partridge

Pigeon rôti
Roast pigeon

Piperade
Cooked tomatoes and pimentos with an omelette mixture added

Pommes (de terre) allumettes
Matchstick potatoes

Pommes (de terre) à l'anglaise
Boiled potatoes

Pommes dauphine
Potato balls covered in choux pastry and deep fried

Pommes frites
Chips or French Fries

Pommes rissolées
Small round potatoes cooked in deep fat

Pommes sautées
Boiled potatoes, sliced then fried

Pommes vapeur
Steamed potatoes

Potée
Vegetable soup

Pot au feu
A soup, almost a stew, made from beef and vegetables

Eating & Drinking
Menu Reader

Poule au riz
Boiled chicken and rice

Poulet Basquaise
Chicken pieces cooked with tomatoes, peppers, mushrooms, diced ham and white wine

Poulet à la crème
Fried chicken with mushrooms and cream

Poulet rôti
Roast chicken

Quiche lorraine
Pastry flan filled with bacon, eggs and cream mixture

Râble de lièvre
Roast saddle of hare

Ragoût de veau
Stewed veal

Raie au beurre noir
Skate in black butter

Ratatouille Niçoise
Onions, green peppers, courgettes (zucchini), aubergine (eggplant), garlic and tomatoes stewed together. Very good cold.

Ris de veau au beurre noir
Sweetbreads in brown butter sauce

Rognons sautés madère
Sautéd kidneys in madeira sauce

Rôti de boeuf
Roast beef

Rôti de porc
Roast pork

Rôti de veau
Roast veal

Salade Niçoise
Many variations on a famous theme: the basic ingredients are green beans, anchovies, black olives, green peppers.

Salade de tomates
Sliced tomatoes in a vinaigrette sauce

Soufflé
The savoury varieties are the same as for omelettes. Sweet varieties such as chocolate and Grand Marnier should also be tried

Soupe à l'oignon
Onion soup

Soupe de poissons
Fish soup

Steak au poivre
Steak with peppercorns

Steak tartare
Minced raw steak, mixed with raw egg, chopped onion, tartare or Worcester sauce, parsley, capers

Tomates farcies
Stuffed tomatoes

Eating & Drinking
Menu Reader

Tomates à la provençale
Grilled tomatoes steeped in garlic

Tournedos Rossini
Tournedos steak on fried bread with *foie gras* and truffles on top

Tripes à la mode de Caen
Tripe with vegetables, herbs, cider and calvados

Truite à la crème
Trout with cream

Truite aux amandes
Trout with almonds

Veau sauté Marengo
Veal casseroled with white wine, garlic and mushrooms

Cheeses

The cheese course normally comes straight after the main dish in France, while the wine is still on the table.

Bleu de Bresse
One of the milder blue-veined cheeses with a soft mottled texture

Brie
Soft and creamy, one of the best known French cheeses

Camembert
Probably the best known cheese of all. Soft and well flavoured, it is pungent when fully ripened

Cantal
Semi-hard, fairly strong flavoured cheese

Carré de l'est
Mild tasting cheese with a flowery rind, best eaten between November and May

Chèvre
Goat's milk cheese: it comes in many varieties and shapes

Comté
A hard cheese from Jura, with a tangy taste

Coulommiers
Similar to *Brie*, soft and creamy

Emmenthal
From Switzerland, but also made in France, a hard cheese with larger holes than *Gruyère*, often used in cooking

Gruyère
A hard Swiss cheese with a delicate flavour

Livarot
Strong-flavoured soft cheese

Petit Suisse
Small pots of rich creamy soft cheese, usually eaten with sugar

Pont-l'évêque
Softish, mature, square-shaped cheese

Reblochon
Soft, mild-flavoured cheese of buttery consistency

Roquefort
Blue-veined cheese made from ewe's milk. Rich and pungent with a crumbly texture

Saint Paulin
Large round cheese made from rich cow's milk

Tomme aux raisins
Semi-soft cheese covered with grape pips

Desserts

Baba au rhum
Sweet, spongy, yeast cake soaked in a rum-flavoured syrup

Beignets de pommes
Apple fritters

Clafoutis
Pastry or batter pudding filled with black cherries

Crème caramel
Caramel custard

Crème renversée
Caramelized custard

Crêpes
Pancakes

Gauffres
Waffles

Glace
Ice-cream. Some varieties are:
au café – coffee
au chocolat – chocolate
au praliné – almonds and burnt sugar crushed up when cold
à la vanille – vanilla

Millefeuille
Layers of wafer-thin puff pastry, filled with cream and raspberry jam

Mousse au chocolat
Chocolate mousse

Pêche melba
Vanilla ice-cream with peaches, raspberry syrup and whipped cream

Sorbet
Water ice or sherbet

Soufflé
The sweet varieties include:
soufflé au chocolat – chocolate
soufflé au Grand Marnier – orange liqueur

Tarte aux fraises
Strawberry flan

Tarte aux pommes
Apple flan

Yaourt
Yoghurt is often eaten as a dessert in France

Eating & Drinking
The Wine List

Here we can only list some of the big names that are likely to be on any wine list. *Un vin en carafe* – a house wine is likely to be very respectable, and it is also worth trying the local wine, *le vin du pays*.

Barsac
Akin to Sauternes, very good sweet white wines

Beaujolais
The most prolific wine area of Burgundy, gives light and fruity wines to be drunk young

Blanc de Blancs
Any white wine made from white grapes only, especially sparkling champagne made this way

Blanquette de Limoux
Dry sparkling white wine from south-west France

Bourgogne
Burgundy

Bourgueil
Light, fruity, deep-coloured red wine from the Loire

Chablis
Dry white Burgundy; firm bodied and clean

Chambertin
A rich, strong Burgundy

Champagne
No comment needed

Châteauneuf du Pape
Full-bodied red Rhône wines

Côte de Beaune
The southern half of the Côte d'Or, Burgundy's best wine area

Côtes du Rhône
Good-bodied Rhône wines

Fleurie
Another great Beaujolais

Gevrey-Chambertin
Full red wine commune of the Côtes de Nuits

Gewürztraminer
Excellent spicy white wine from Alsace

Jasnières
Light, medium-sweet Loire white wines

Juliénas
A fine Beaujolais

Mâcon
Good ordinary red and white Burgundy

Margaux
A fine lightish red wine from Bordeaux

Eating & Drinking
The Wine List

Médoc
The principal red wine area of Bordeaux

Meursault
Fine dry white Burgundy

Monbazillac
Sweet white wine from the Dordogne

Moulin à Vent
Another fine Beaujolais

Muscadet
Very dry white wine from the Loire

Pauillac
Wines from the best commune of Bordeaux for red wines, in the northern Médoc

Pomerol
A full red Bordeaux

Pouilly-Fuissé
Good white Burgundy, light and dry

Pouilly-Fumé
Flinty, spicy, dry white Loire wine

Riesling
Clean and scented Alsace wine

Rosé d'Anjou
Pink wine from the Loire Valley

Saint-Amour
A full red Beaujolais

Saint-Émilion
A fine red Bordeaux

Sancerre
Dry, stony, delicate white Loire wine

Sauternes
A good, sometimes great, sweet white wine

Sylvaner
Dry white wine from Alsace

Volnay
Lightish red Burgundy with a fine bouquet

Vouvray
Fine white Loire wine, medium-dry to medium-sweet

In the Café

The French café is an institution – sit on the terrace and watch the world go by while you have breakfast, an apéritif or a coffee after dinner. Many sell snacks and some serve complete meals. It's a place to telephone (phrases page 100), and often to buy stamps and cigarettes: you'll find a counter where these are sold if there's a red diamond-shaped *TABAC* sign outside. You usually pay for your drinks when you leave, not when they arrive, and remember to check if service is included. But first, how to order:

un verre de rouge *uñ ver duh roozh*	a glass of red wine	**un verre de blanc** *uñ ver duh bloñ*	a glass of white wine
une bière en bouteille *ōōn byer oñ boo-tay*	a bottle of beer	**un demi** *uñ duh-mee*	a glass of beer
		un whisky *uñ wee-skee*	a whisky
un cognac *uñ kon-yak*	a brandy	**un martini** *uñ mar-tee-nee*	a martini

You may prefer to try something more characteristically French:

un pastis   an aniseed drink, taken with water and ice
uñ pas-tees

or one of the bitter herb apéritifs, such as

un Ambassadeur   **un Dubonnet**
uñ noñ-ba-sa-dur   *uñ dōō-bo-nay*

and after dinner you could try a special brandy:

un marc   **un armagnac**
uñ mar   *uñ nar-man-yak*

You may want something hot like

un café *uñ ka-fay*	a black coffee	**un café-crème** *uñ ka-fay-krem*	coffee with milk
un thé au lait *uñ '*	tea with milk	**un chocolat chaud** *uñ sho-kō-la shō*	hot chocolate

If you want a soft drink for yourself or the children, you can ask for·

un jus d'orange – an orange juice
uñ zhōō do-roñzh

un jus de pamplemousse – a grapefruit juice
uñ zhōō duh poñ-pluh-moos

un jus d'ananas – a pineapple juice
uñ zhōō da-na-na

un Orangina – an orangeade drink
uñ no-roñ-zhee-na

un Perrier – a sparkling mineral water
uñ pe-ree-yay

une fraise – a strawberry fruit cordial
ōōn frez

une menthe – a mint-flavoured cordial
ōōn moñt

In the morning, ask for a croissant (*uñ krwah-soñ*) with your coffee; if you're hungry later in the day you may be able to get snacks such as·

un sandwich ... au fromage – a cheese sandwich
uñ soñd-veetch ... ō fro-mazh

... au jambon – a ham sandwich
... ō zhoñ-boñ

... au pâté – a pâté sandwich
... ō pa-tay

... au saucisson – a salami sandwich
... ō sō-see-soñ

des chips – potato crisps (chips)
day cheep

un œuf dur – a hard-boiled egg
uñ nuf dōōr

un croque-monsieur – toasted ham and cheese open sandwich
uñ krok-muh-syuh

un œuf jambon – ham and egg
uñ nuf zhoñ-boñ

Paying

How much is that?	– C'est combien? *say koñ-byeñ?*
I can't afford that much	– C'est trop cher pour moi *say trõ sher poor mwah*
What does that come to?	– Ça fait combien en tout? *sa fe koñ-byeñ oñ too?*
Are service and tax included?	– Le service et le TVA sont compris? *luh ser-vees ay luh tay-vay-ah soñ koñ-pree?*

How much is it
C'est combien
say koñ-byeñ

– **to get in?**
l'entrée?
loñ-tray?

– **for a child?**
pour un enfant?
poor uñ noñ-foñ?

– **to phone to Britain?**
pour téléphoner en Grande-Bretagne?
poor tay-lay-fõ-nay oñ groñd bruh-tan-yuh?

How much is it
C'est combien
say koñ-byeñ

– **per person?**
par personne?
par per-son?

– **per night?**
la nuit?
la nwee?

– **per kilo?**
le kilo?
luh kee-lõ?

– **per metre?**
le mètre?
luh met-ruh?

– **per kilometre?**
le kilomètre?
luh kee-lõ-met-ruh?

Is there any extra charge? – Est-ce qu'il y a des suppléments?
es-keel ya day sõo-play-moñ?

Is there a reduction for – **a group?**
Est-ce qu'il y a une réduction   un groupe?
pour
es-keel ya ōōn ray-dōōx-yoñ poor   *uñ groop?*

– **students?**
les étudiants?
lay zay-tōōd-yoñ?

– **senior citizens?**
le troisième âge?
luh trwah-zyem azh?

Do I pay a deposit? – Est-ce que vous exigez des arrhes?
es-kuh voo zeg-zee-zhay day zar?

Do I pay in advance or – Est-ce que je paie d'avance ou après?
afterwards?   *es-kuh zhuh pay da-voñs oo a-pre?*

Do you accept traveller's – Est-ce que vous acceptez les chèques
cheques?   de voyage?
es-kuh voo zax-ep-tay lay shek duh
vwah-yazh?

I want to pay by credit card – Je désire payer avec une carte de crédit
zhuh day-zeer pa-yay a-vek ōōn kart duh
kray-dee

Can I have an itemized bill? – Est-ce que je peux avoir une addition
avec le détail?
es-kuh zhuh puh za-vwar ōōn a-dee-syoñ
a-vek luh day-tye?

Can I have a receipt? – Est-ce que je peux avoir un reçu?
es-kuh zhuh puh za-vwar uñ ruh-sōō?

You've given me the wrong – Vous avez fait une erreur en me rendant
change   la monnaie
voo za-vay fe tōōn e-rur oñ muh roñ-doñ la
mo-nay

Please send it to this address – Expédiez cela à cette adresse s'il vous
plaît
ex-paya-yay sla a set a-dres see voo play

Please pack it carefully – Emballez cela avec soin, s'il vous plaît
oñ-ba-lay sla a-vek swañ see voo play

The Basic Phrases

Whatever it is you want to buy you'll need some of these phrases.

I would like – **a box of matches**
Je voudrais   une boîte d'allumettes
zhuh voo-dre   *zōōn bwaht da-lōō-met*

– **some stamps**
des timbres
day tañ-bruh

Do you sell sunglasses? – Est-ce que vous vendez des lunettes de soleil?
es-kuh voo voñ-day day lōō-net duh so-lay?

Have you got any – **English newspapers?**
Est-ce que vous avez   des journaux anglais?
es-kuh voo za-vay   *day zhoor-nō zoñ-glay?*

– **toothpaste?**
du dentifrice?
dōō doñ-tee-frees?

I need some suntan oil – J'ai besoin d'huile solaire
zhay buh-zwañ dweel so-ler

Where is – **the shoe department?**
Où est   le rayon des chaussures?
oo ay   *luh ray-yoñ day shō-sōōr?*

– **the food department?**
le rayon d'alimentation?
luh ray-yoñ da-lee-moñ-tas-yoñ?

Can I see – **the hat in the window?**
Est-ce que je peux voir   le chapeau en vitrine?
es-kuh zhuh puh vwar   *luh sha-pō oñ vee-treen?*

– **that hat over there?**
ce chapeau-là?
suh sha-pō la?

No, the other one – Non, l'autre
noñ, lō-truh

Have you got anything – Est-ce que vous avez quelque chose de
cheaper?   moins cher?
es-kuh voo za-vay kel-kuh-shōz duh mwañ sher?

The Basic Phrases

Have you got – **a larger one?**
Est-ce que vous en avez un plus grand?
es-kuh voo zoñ na-vay *uñ plōō groñ?*

– **a smaller one?**
un plus petit?
uñ plōō puh-tee?

I'm just looking – Je regarde seulement
zhuh ruh-gard suhl-moñ

I'm looking for a blouse – Je cherche un chemisier
zhuh shersh un shuh-meez-yay

I like this one – J'aime celui-ci
zhem suh-lwee-see

I don't like it – Je n'aime pas celui-là
zhuh nem pa suh-lwee-la

I'll take – **this one**
Je prendrai celui-ci
zhuh proñ-dray *suh-lwee-see*

– **that one**
celui-là
suh-lwee-la

– **the other one**
l'autre
lō-truh

Please wrap it – Est-ce que vous pouvez me l'envelopper,
s'il vous plaît?
es-kuh voo poo-vay muh loñ-vlo-pay, see voo play?

There's no need to wrap it, thank you – Inutile de l'envelopper, merci
ee-nōō-teel duh loñ-vlo-pay, mer-see

Can I have a plastic bag? – Un sac en plastique, s'il vous plaît
uñ sak oñ plas-teek, see voo play

Food

Of course, you can solve all your language problems by heading for the nearest supermarket, but you will miss the personal touch of the shopkeepers and the people in the market.

I'd like – **a kilo of apples (2 lb 3 oz)**
Je voudrais un kilo de pommes
zhuh voo-dre *zuñ kee-lō duh pom*

– **a pound of tomatoes (1 lb 2 oz)**
une livre de tomates
zōōn lee-vruh duh to-mat

– **half a pound of butter (250 gm/9 oz)**
une demi-livre de beurre
zōōn duh-mee lee-vruh duh bur

– **100 gm of ground coffee**
cent grammes de café en grains
soñ gram duh ka-fay oñ grañ

– **5 slices of ham**
cinq tranches de jambon
sañk troñsh duh zhoñ-boñ

– **half a dozen eggs**
six œufs
see zuh

A bag of sugar please – Un paquet de sucre, s'il vous plaît
uñ pa-kay duh sōō-kruh, see voo play

A litre of milk, please – Un litre de lait, s'il vous plaît
uñ lee-truh duh lay, see voo play

A bottle of wine please – Une bouteille de vin, s'il vous plaît
ōōn boo-tay duh vañ, see voo play

2 pork chops, please – Deux côtès de porc, s'il vous plaît
duh kōt duh por, see voo play

A lamb joint, please – Un rôti d'agneau, s'il vous plaît
uñ rō-tee dan-yō, see voo play

A steak, please – Un steak, s'il vous plaît
uñ stek, see voo play

Food
Meat & Groceries

MEAT

beef	le bœuf *luh buf*	**liver**	le foie *luh fwah*
chicken	le poulet *luh poo-lay*	**kidneys**	les rognons *lay roñ-nyoñ*
ham	le jambon *luh zhoñ-boñ*	**pork**	le porc *luh por*
lamb	l'agneau *lan-yō*	**veal**	le veau *luh vō*

GROCERIES

baby food	les petits pots (pour enfant) *lay puh-tee pō (poor oñ-foñ)*	**mustard**	la moutarde *la moo-tard*
		oil	l'huile *lweel*
bread	le pain *luh pañ*	**pepper**	le poivre *luh pwah-vruh*
butter	le beurre *luh bur*	**rice**	le riz *luh ree*
cheese	le fromage *luh fro-mazh*	**salt**	le sel *luh sel*
coffee	le café *luh ka-fay*	**soup**	la soupe *la soop*
cream	la crème *la krem*	**sugar**	le sucre *luh sōō-kruh*
eggs	les œufs *lay zuh*	**tea**	le thé *luh tay*
flour	la farine *la fa-reen*	**vinegar**	le vinaigre *luh vee-neg-ruh*
jam	la confiture *la koñ-ſee-tōōr*	**yoghurt**	le yaourt *luh ya-oor*
milk	le lait *luh lay*		

Food
Fish & Fruit

FISH

crayfish	les langoustines *lay loñ-goo-steen*	**pike**	le brochet *luh bro-she*
hake	le colin *luh ko-lañ*	**sea bream**	la daurade *la dō-rad*
John Dory	la dorée *la do-ray*	**shad**	l'alose *la-lōz*
lobster	le homard *luh ō-mar*	**sole**	la sole *la sol*
oysters	les huîtres *layz wee-truh*	**trout**	ła truite *la trweet*
perch	la perche *la persh*	**turbot**	le turbot *luh tōōr-bō*

FRUIT

apples	les pommes *lay pom*	**oranges**	les oranges *lay zo-roñzh*
apricots	les abricots *lay za-bree-kō*	**peach**	la pêche *la pesh*
bananas	les bananes *lay ba-nan*	**pears**	les poires *lay pwahr*
cherries	les cerises *lay suh-reez*	**pineapple**	l'ananas *la-na-na*
grapefruit	le pamplemousse *luh poñ-pluh-moos*	**plums**	les prunes *lay prōōn*
grapes	les raisins *lay ray-zañ*	**pomegranate**	la grenadine *la gruh-na-deen*
lemon	le citron *luh see-troñ*	**raspberries**	les framboises *lay froñ-bwahz*
melon	le melon *luh muh-loñ*	**strawberries**	les fraises *lay frez*
olives	les olives *lay zo-leev*	**watermelon**	la pastèque *la pas-tek*

Food
Vegetables & Herbs

artichoke	l'artichaut *lar-tee-shō*	**leek**	le poireau *luh pwah-rō*
asparagus	les asperges *lay zas-perzh*	**lettuce**	la laitue *la lay-tōō*
aubergine	l'aubergine *lō-ber-zheen*	**mint**	la menthe *la moñt*
avocado	l'avocat *la-vō-ka*	**mushrooms**	les champignons *lay shoñ-peen-yoñ*
beetroot	la betterave *la bet-rav*	**onions**	les oignons *lay zoñ-nyoñ*
carrots	les carottes *lay ka-rot*	**parsley**	le persil *luh per-see*
cauliflower	le chou-fleur *luh shoo-flur*	**peas**	les petits pois *lay puh-tee pwah*
celery	le céleri *luh sayl-ree*	**potatoes**	les pommes de terre *lay pom duh ter*
chicory	l'endive *loñ-deev*	**radishes**	les radis *lay ra-dee*
chives	la ciboulette *la see-boo-let*	**red pepper**	le poivron rouge *luh pwah-vroñ roozh*
courgettes	les courgettes *lay koor-zhet*	**sage**	la sauge *la sōzh*
cucumber	le concombre *le koñ-koñ-bruh*	**shallots**	les échalotes *lay zay-sha-lot*
eggplant	l'aubergine *lō-ber-zheen*	**spinach**	les épinards *lay zay-pee-nar*
French beans	les haricots verts *lay a-ree-kō ver*	**tarragon**	l'estragon *les-tra-goñ*
garlic	l'ail *lye*	**tomatoes**	les tomates *lay to-mat*
green pepper	le poivron vert *luh pwah-vroñ ver*	**zucchini**	les courgettes *lay koor-zhet*

Newspapers & Stationery

If you want a newspaper, you'll get it at a news stand, *un kiosque à journaux*, while stationery is generally sold along with books in a *librairie-papeterie*.

Have you got any Est-ce que vous avez *es kuh voo za-vay*	**– English newspapers?** des journaux anglais? *day zhoor-nō zoñ-glay?*
	– American newspapers? des journaux américains? *day zhoor-nō za-may-ree-kañ?*
	– postcards? des cartes postales? *day kart po-stal?*
I would like Je voudrais *zhuh voo-dre*	**– some notepaper** du papier à lettres *dōō pap-yay a le-truh*
	– some envelopes des enveloppes *day zoñ-vlop*
	– a pen un stylo *zuñ stee-lō*
	– a pencil un crayon *zuñ kray-yoñ*
I need J'ai besoin *zhay buh-zwañ*	**– a bottle of ink** d'une bouteille d'encre *dōōn boo-tay doñ-kruh*
	– some adhesive tape de Scotch *duh skotch*
Do you sell Est-ce que vous vendez *es-kuh voo voñ-day*	**– English paperbacks?** des livres de poches anglais? *day lee-vruh duh posh oñ-glay?*
	– street maps? des plans de la ville? *day ploñ duh la veel?*

Although there are some little shops whose main business is selling tobacco, a *café-tabac,* that is a café with a red *TABAC* sign outside, is the easiest place to buy it. British and American brands of cigarettes are often available along with the stronger French varieties. Don't forget that wherever tobacco is sold you can also buy stamps; you will find the phrases you want in the Post Office section on page 99.

A packet of . . . please	– Un paquet de . . . s'il vous plaît *uñ pa-ke duh . . . see voo play*
with filter-tip	– avec filtre *a-vek feel-truh*
without filter	– sans filtre *soñ feel-truh*
Have you got any American brands?	– Est-ce que vous avez des cigarettes américaines? *es-kuh voo za-vay day see-ga-ret a-may-ree-ken?*
Have you got any English brands?	– Est-ce que vous avez des cigarettes anglaises? *es-kuh voo za-vay day see-ga-ret oñ-glez?*
A pouch of pipe tobacco	– Du tabac pour pipe *dōō ta-ba poor peep*
Some pipe cleaners	– Un cure-pipe *uñ kōōr-peep*
A box of matches	– Une boîte d'allumettes *ōōn bwaht da-lōō-met*
A cigar	– Un cigare *uñ see-gar*
A cigarette lighter	– Un briquet *uñ bree-ke*
A gas (butane) refill	– Une recharge de briquet *ōōn ruh-sharzh duh bree-ke*

The Chemist/Druggist

You should see the *If You're Ill* section if anybody is really unwell, but a chemist should be able to help you with minor ailments. There will be an illuminated green cross outside. He might not sell the range of toiletries stocked by chemists at home, and he certainly won't sell film – for that you want a photographic shop.

I want something for – **a headache**
Je voudrais quelque chose pour   un mal de tête
  zhuh voo-dre kel-kuh-shōz poor   *uñ mal duh tet*

         – **insect bites**
         les piqûres d'insectes
         lay pee-kōōr dañ-sekt

How many do I take? – J'en prends combien?
      zhoñ proñ koñ-byeñ?

How often do I take them? – Combien de fois par jour faut-il les
      prendre?
      *koñ-byeñ duh fwah par zhoor fō-teel lay
      proñ-druh?*

Are they safe for children to – Est-ce que les enfants peuvent en
        take?   prendre?
      es-kuh lay zoñ-foñ puhv toñ proñ-druh?

You might also want something for:

chapped skin	les gerçures *lay zher-sōōr*	**a sore throat**	un mal de gorge *uñ mal duh gorzh*
a cold	un rhume *uñ rōōm*	**sunburn**	un coup de soleil *uñ koo duh so-lay*
a cough	la toux *la too*	**toothache**	une rage de dents *ōōn razh duh doñ*
hay fever	le rhume des foins *luh rōōm day fwañ*	**an upset stomach**	un mal d'estomac *uñ mal des-to-ma*

or need some of the items on the next page.

The Chemist/Druggist

aftershave	la lotion après-rasage *la lō-syoñ a-pre ra-zazh*	lipstick	le rouge à lèvres *luh roozh a lev-ruh*
antiseptic	l'antiseptique *loñ-tee-sep-teek*	mascara	le mascara *luh mas-ka-ra*
aspirin	l'aspirine *las-pee-reen*	mouthwash	l'eau dentifrice *lō doñ-tee-frees*
bandage	le pansement *luh poñs-moñ*	nail file	la lime à ongles *la leem a oñ-gluh*
band-aid	le sparadrap *luh spa-ra-dra*	nail varnish	le vernis à ongles *luh ver-nee a oñ-gluh*
bubble bath	le bain moussant *lüh bañ moo-soñ*	nail varnish remover	le dissolvant *luh dee-sol-voñ*
cleansing milk	le lait démaquillant *luh lay day-ma-kee-yoñ*	perfume	le parfum *luh par-fuñ*
contraceptive	le contraceptif *luh koñ-tra-sep-teef*	powder	la poudre *la poo-druh*
cotton wool	le coton *luh ko-toñ*	razor blades	les lames de rasoir *lay lam duh ra-zwar*
deodorant	le déodorant corporel *luh day-ō-dō-roñ kor-por-el*	rouge	le rouge à joues *luh roozh a zhoo*
disinfectant	le désinfectant *luh day-zañ-fek-toñ*	sanitary towels (napkins)	les serviettes hygiéniques *lay ser-vyet ee-zhay-neek*
eye shadow	le fard à paupières *luh far da pō-pyer*	shampoo	le shampooing *luh shoñ-pwañ*
hair spray	la laque *la lak*	shaving cream	la crème à raser *la krem a ra-zay*
hand cream	la crème pour les mains *la krem poor lay mañ*	soap	le savon *luh sa-voñ*
insect repellant	la crème anti-insecte *la krem oñ-tee añ-sekt*	suntan oil	l'huile solaire *lweel so-ler*
		talc	le talc *luh talk*
Kleenex	le Kleenex *luh klee-nex*	toilet water	l'eau de toilette *lō duh twah-let*
laxative	le laxatif *luh lax-a-teef*	toothbrush	la brosse à dents *la bros a doñ*
		toothpaste	le dentifrice *luh doñ-tee-frees*

Camera Shop

I need a film – **for this camera**
J'ai besoin d'un film   pour cet appareil-photo
zhay buh-zwañ duñ feelm   *poor set a-pa-ray fō-tō*

– **for this cine-camera**
pour cette caméra
poor set ka-may-ra

I want – **a black and white film**
Je voudrais   une pellicule noir et blanc
zhuh voo-dre   *zōōn pe-lee-kōōl nwar ay bloñ*

– **a colour print film**
une pellicule couleur sur papier
zōōn pe-lee-kōōl koo-lur sōōr pap-yay

– **a colour slide film**
une pellicule couleur pour diapositives
zōōn pe-lee-kōōl koo-lur poor dee-a-poz-ee-teev

– **batteries for the flash**
des piles pour le flash
day peel poor luh flash

Can you develop this film – Est-ce que vous pouvez développer ce
please?   film s'il vous plaît?
es-kuh voo poo-vay day-vlo-pay suh feelm see voo play?

I would like 2 prints of this – Je voudrais cette photo en deux
one   exemplaires
zhuh voo-dre set fō-tō oñ duh zeg-zoñ-pler

When will the photos be – Quand est-ce que les photos seront
ready?   prêtes?
koñ tes-kuh lay fō-tō suh-roñ pret?

I would like this photo – Je voudrais un agrandissement de cette
enlarged   photo
zhuh voo-dre zuñ na-groñ-dees-moñ duh set fō-tō

There is something wrong – Mon appareil-photo marche mal
with my camera   *moñ na-pa-ray fō-tō marsh mal*

The film is jammed – Le film est bloqué dans l'appareil
luh feelm ay blo-kay doñ la-pay-ray

Camera Shop
Accessories

accessory	l'accessoire *lax-es-war*	negative	le négatif *luh nay-ga-teef*
blue filter	le filtre bleu *luh feel-truh bluh*	over-exposed	surexposé *sōōr-ex-pō-zay*
cartridge	le chargeur *luh shar-zhur*	picture	la photo *la fō-tō*
cassette	la cassette *la ka-set*	print	la photo sur papier *la fō-tō sōōr pap-yay*
cine-camera	la caméra *la ka-may-ra*	projector	le projecteur *luh pro-zhek-tur*
distance	la distance *la dee-stoñs*	red filter	le filtre rouge *luh feel-truh roozh*
enlargement	l'agrandissement *la-groñ-dees-moñ*	reel	la pellicule *la pe-lee-kōōl*
exposure	la pose *la pōz*	rewind mechanism	le système de rembobinage *luh see-stem duh roñ-bo-bee-nazh*
exposure meter	le pose-mètre *luh pōz-me-truh*		
flash	le flash *luh flash*	shade	l'ombre *loñ-bruh*
flash bulbs	les ampoules de flash *lay zoñ-pool duh flash*	shutter	l'obturateur *lob-tōō-ra-tur*
flash cubes	les flashs cubes *lay flash kōōb*	shutter speed	la vitesse d'obturation *la vee-tes dob-tōō-ras-yoñ*
focal distance	la distance focale *la dee-stoñs fō-kal*	slide	la diapo *la dee-ya-pō*
focus	le foyer *luh fwa-yay*	tripod	le trépied *luh tray-pyay*
in focus	au point *ō pwañ*	under-exposed	sous-exposé *soo-zex-pō-zay*
out of focus	pas au point *pa zō pwañ*	viewfinder	le viseur *luh vee-zur*
image	l'image *lee-mazh*	wide-angle lens	la lentille grand-angle *la loñ-tee groñ-toñ-gluh*
lens	la lentille *la loñ-tee*		
lens cover	le protège-lentille *luh pro-tezh loñ-tee*	yellow filter	le filtre jaune *luh feel-truh zhōn*
movie camera	la caméra *la ka-may-ra*		

Clothes Sizes

First of all you'll want some idea of your continental size. Unfortunately slight variations in sizes mean that these can only be approximate equivalents.

Dresses

UK	10	12	14	16	18
US	8	10	12	14	16
France	36	38	40	42	44

Ladies' sweaters

UK/US	32	34	36	38	40
France	36	38	40	42	44

Ladies' shoes

UK	3	$3\frac{1}{2}$	4	$4\frac{1}{2}$	5	$5\frac{1}{2}$	6	$6\frac{1}{2}$
US	$4\frac{1}{2}$	5	$5\frac{1}{2}$	6	$6\frac{1}{2}$	7	$7\frac{1}{2}$	8
France	35	36	37	$37\frac{1}{2}$	38	$38\frac{1}{2}$	39	40

Men's shoes

UK	7	8	9	10	11
US	$8\frac{1}{2}$	$9\frac{1}{2}$	$10\frac{1}{2}$	$11\frac{1}{2}$	$12\frac{1}{2}$
France	$40\frac{1}{2}$	42	43	44	$45\frac{1}{2}$

Clothes Sizes

Sometimes men's clothing has the appropriate measurement in centimetres, sometimes it has a size which is half that centimetre measurement. So, for instance, if you want a pair of trousers and you have a 32 inch waist, you will want either an 80 centimetre waist or a size 40.

Waist and chest measurements

inches	28	30	32	34	36	38	40
centimetres	71	76	80	87	91	97	102

inches	42	44	46	48	50	52	54
centimetres	107	112	117	122	127	132	138

Men's shirts

UK/US	14	14½	15	15½	16	16½	17
France	36	37	38	39	41	42	43

Clothes

I would like Je voudrais *zhuh voo-dre*	**– a dress** une robe *zōōn rob*
	– a sweater un pull *zuñ pōōl*
I take a continental size 40	– Je porte du quarante *zhuh port dōō ka-roñt*
I take a continental shoe size 40	– Je chausse du quarante *zhuh shōs dōō ka-roñt*
Can you measure me?	– Est-ce que vous pouvez prendre mes mesures? *es-kuh voo poo-vay proñ-druh may muh-zōōr?*
Have you got this in blue?	– Est-ce que vous l'avez en bleu? *es-kuh voo la-vay zoñ bluh?*
What is the material?	– C'est fait en quoi? *say fet oñ kwah?*
I like J'aime *zhem*	**– this one** celui-ci *suh-lwee-see*
	– that one there celui-là *suh-lwee-la*
	– the one in the window celui qui est en vitrine *suh-lwee kee et oñ vee-treen*
May I take it over to the light?	– Est-ce que je peux le regarder au jour? *es-kuh zhuh puh luh ruh-gar-day ō zhoor?*
May I try it on?	– Est-ce que je peux l'essayer? *es-kuh zhuh puh le-say-yay?*
Where are the changing (dressing) rooms?	– Où sont les cabines d'essayage? *oo soñ lay ka-been de-say-yazh?*
I want a mirror	– Je voudrais une glace *zhuh voo-dre zōōn glas*

I like it – J'aime ça
zhem sa

I don't like it – Je n'aime pas ça
zhuh nem pa sa

It doesn't fit – Cela ne me va pas
sla nuh muh va pa

It's – **too big**
C'est   trop grand
say   *trō groñ*

   – **too small**
   trop petit
   trō puh-tee

I'd like one – **with a zip**
J'en voudrais un   avec une fermeture éclair
zhoñ voo-dre zuñ   *a-vek ōōn fer-muh-tōōr ay-kler*

   – **without a belt**
   sans ceinture
   soñ sañ-tōōr

Is this all you have? – Est-ce que c'est tout ce que vous avez?
es-kuh say toos kuh voo za-vay?

I'll take it – Je le prends
zhuh luh proñ

Is it washable? – Est-ce que c'est lavable?
es-kuh say la-va-bluh?

Will it shrink? – Est-ce que ça rétrécit au lavage?
es-kuh sa ray-tray-see ō la-vazh?

Must it be dry-cleaned? – Est-ce qu'il faut le nettoyer à sec?
es-keel fō luh net-wah-yay a sek?

Clothes

blouse	le chemisier *luh shuh-meez-yay*	**shorts**	le short *luh short*
bra	le soutien-gorge *luh soo-tyeñ gorzh*	**skirt**	la jupe *la zhoop*
cardigan	le cardigan *luh kar-dee-goñ*	**slip**	la combinaison *la koñ-bee-ne-zoñ*
coat	le manteau *luh moñ-tō*	**sneakers**	les chaussures de tennis *lay shō-soor duh te-nees*
dress	la robe *la rob*		
dungarees	la salopette *la sa-lo-pet*	**socks**	les chaussettes *lay shō-set*
gloves	les gants *lay goñ*	**stockings**	les bas *lay bah*
hat	le chapeau *luh sha-pō*	**suit (man's)**	le costume *luh kos-tōōm*
jacket	la veste *la vest*	**suit (woman's)**	le tailleur *luh tye-yur*
jeans	les jeans *lay jeen*	**sweater**	le pull *luh pōōl*
nightdress	la chemise de nuit *la shuh-meez duh nwee*	**swimming trunks**	le slip de bain *luh sleep duh bañ*
panties	la petite culotte *la puh-teet kōō-lot*	**swimsuit**	le maillot de bain *luh mye-yō duh bañ*
petticoat	le jupon *luh zhōō-poñ*	**tie**	la cravate *la kra-vat*
pullover	le pull *luh pōōl*	**tights**	le collant *luh ko-loñ*
pyjamas	le pyjama *luh pee-zha-ma*	**towel**	la serviette *la serv-yet*
raincoat	l'imperméable *lañ-per-may-ah-bluh*	**trousers**	le pantalon *luh poñ-ta-loñ*
sandals	les sandales *lay-soñ-dal*	**T shirt**	le T shirt *luh tee-shert*
scarf	l'écharpe *lay-sharp*	**underpants**	le slip *luh sleep*
shirt	la chemise *la shuh-meez*	**vest**	le gilet de corps *luh zhee-lay duh kor*

MATERIALS

acrylic	l'acrylique
	lak-ree-leek
corduroy	le velours côtelé
	luh vuh-loor kôt-lay
cotton	le coton
	luh ko-toñ
denim	le jean
	luh jeen
easy-care fabric	tissu d'entretien facile
	tee-sōō doñ-truh-tyeñ fa-seel
fur	la fourrure
	la foo-rōōr
jersey	le jersey
	luh jer-zay
lace	la dentelle
	la doñ-tel
leather	le cuir
	luh kweer
linen	le lin
	luh lañ
nylon	le nylon
	luh nee-loñ
polyester	le polyester
	luh pol-yes-ter
poplin	la popeline
	la pop-leen
rayon	la rayonne
	la ray-yon
silk	la soie
	la swah
suede	le daim
	luh dañ
terylene	le tergal
	luh ter-gal
velvet	le velours
	luh vuh-loor
wool	la laine
	la len

ACCESSORIES

belt	la ceinture
	la sañ-tōōr
bracelet	le bracelet
	luh bras-lay
brooch	la broche
	la brosh
button	le bouton
	luh boo-toñ
earrings	les boucles d'oreille
	lay boo-kluh do-ray
handbag	le sac à main
	luh sak a mañ
handkerchief	le mouchoir
	luh moo-shwar
necklace	le collier
	luh kol-yay
pendant	le pendentif
	luh poñ-doñ-teef
purse	(UK) le porte-monnaie
	luh port mo-nay
	(US) le sac à main
	luh sak a mañ
ring	la bague
	la bag
umbrella	le parapluie
	luh pa-ra-plwee
wallet	le porte-feuille
	luh port-fye
watch	la montre
	la moñ-truh
zip	la fermeture éclair
	la fer-muh-tōōr ay-kler

The Hairdresser

I'd like to make an – Je voudrais prendre rendez-vous
appointment *zhuh voo-dre proñ-druh roñ-day-voo*

I want – **a cut**
Je voudrais   une coupe simple
zhuh voo-dre   *zōon koop sañ-pluh*

– **a trim**
un rafraîchissement
zuñ ra-fre-shees-moñ

– **a blow-dry**
un brushing
zuñ bruh-sheeng

I want my hair – **fairly short**
Je voudrais les cheveux coupés   assez courts
zhuh voo-dre lay shuh-vuh koo-pay   *a-say koor*

– **not too short**
pas trop courts
pa trō koor

– **short and curly**
courts et frisés
koor ay free-zay

– **layered**
en dégradé
oñ day-gra-day

– **in a fringe**
avec une frange
a-vek ōon froñzh

Take more off – **the front**
Coupez-en davantage   devant
koo-pay zoñ da-voñ-tazh   *duh-voñ*

– **the back**
derrière
der-yer

Not too much off – **the sides**
Pas trop dégagé   sur les côtés
pa trō day-ga-zhay   *sōor lay kō-tay*

– **the top**
sur le dessus
sōor luh duh-sōo

The Hairdresser

I'd like	**– a perm (permanent)**
Je voudrais	une permanente
zhuh voo-dre	*zōōn per-ma-noñt*
	– a curly perm
	une permanente bouclée
	zōōn per-ma-noñt boo-klay
	– a shampoo and set
	un shampooing mise en plis
	zuñ shoñ-pwañ meez oñ plee
	– my hair tinted
	une coloration
	zōōn ko-lo-ras-yoñ
	– my hair streaked
	des mèches
	day mesh
The water is too hot	**– L'eau est trop chaude**
	lō ay trō shōd
The dryer is too hot	**– Le séchoir est trop chaud**
	luh say-shwar ay trō shō
I'd like	**– a conditioner**
Je voudrais	un après-shampooing
zhuh voo-dre	*zuñ na-pre-shoñ-pwañ*
	– hair spray
	de la laque
	duh la lak
That's fine thank you	**– C'est très bien merci**
	say tray byeñ mer-see

Dry Cleaners & Laundry

A dry cleaner's is called either *une teinturerie* or *un pressing;* sometimes it is combined with *une blanchisserie* or laundry which will usually provide a fairly quick service. If you don't mind the chore of doing the washing yourself, you should look for *une laverie automatique.*

Will you – **clean this skirt?**
Pouvez-vous nettoyer cette jupe?
poo-vay voo net-wah-yay set zhoop?

– **press these trousers?**
repasser ce pantalon?
ruh-pa-say suh poñ-ta-loñ?

– **wash and iron these shirts?**
laver et repasser ces chemises?
la-vay ay ruh-pa-say say shuh-meez?

– **wash these clothes?**
laver ces affaires?
la-vay say za-fer?

This stain is – **grease**
Ceci, c'est une tache de graisse
suh-see, set oon tash duh gres

– **ink**
d'encre
doñ-kruh

– **coffee**
de café
duh ka-fay

This fabric is delicate – C'est un tissu délicat
set uñ tee-soo day-lee-ka

When will my things be ready? – Quand est-ce que mes affaires seront prêtes?
koñ tes-kuh may za-fer suh-roñ pret?

I need them in a hurry – Je les voudrais assez rapidement
zhuh lay voo-dre za-say ra-peed-moñ

Is there a launderette nearby? – Est-ce qu'il y a une laverie automatique près d'ici?
es-keel ya oon lav-ree o-to-ma-teek pre dee-see?

I'm having trouble with my camera – J'ai des ennuis avec mon appareil-photo
zhay day zoñ-nwee a-vek moñ na-pa-ray fō-tō

This is – **broken**
C'est   cassé
say   *ka-say*

– **damaged**
endommagé
oñ-dom-a-zhay

– **torn**
déchiré
day-shee-ray

Would you have a look at this please? – Est-ce que vous pouvez regarder cela s'il vous plaît?
es-kuh voo poo-vay ruh-gar-day suh-la see voo play?

Can you fix it? – Est-ce que vous pouvez le réparer?
es-kuh voo poo-vay luh ray-pa-ray?

Can you reheel these shoes? – Est-ce que vous pouvez ressemeler ces chaussures?
es-kuh voo poo-vay ruh-suhm-lay say shō-sōōr?

Have you got a replacement part? – Est-ce que vous avez une pièce de rechange?
es-kuh voo za-vay zōōn pyes duh ruh-shoñzh?

When will it be ready? – Quand est-ce que cela sera prêt?
koñ tes-kuh suh-la suh-ra pre?

Can you do it quickly? – Est-ce que vous pouvez le faire rapidement?
es-kuh voo poo-vay luh fer ra-peed-moñ?

Can you give me – **some strong glue?**
Pouvez-vous me donner   de la colle forte?
poo-vay voo muh do-nay   *duh la kol fort?*

– **some string?**
de la ficelle?
duh la fee-sel?

– **some adhesive tape?**
du Scotch?
dōō skotch?

Banks are usually open from 9 a.m. until 4 p.m. and most close for lunch. You may be told to pick up your currency from a separate desk or *caisse*. You can also change money at hotels, large stores and, of course, *bureaux de change*, but the rate of exchange tends to be less favourable. Those at airports and major railway stations stay open at night and over the weekend.

Will you change – **these traveller's cheques?**
Est-ce que vous pouvez me changer   ces chèques de voyage?
es-kuh voo poo-vay muh shoñ-zhay   *say shek duh vwah-yazh?*

  – **these notes (bills)?**
ces billets?
say bee-yay?

What is the rate for – **sterling?**
À combien est   la livre sterling?
a koñ-byeñ nay   *la lee-vruh ster-leeng?*

  – **dollars?**
le dollar?
luh do-lar?

I would like to cash a cheque with my Eurocheque card – Je voudrais retirer de l'argent avec ma carte eurochèque
zhuh voo-dre ruh-tee-ray duh lar-zhoñ a-vek ma kart ur-rō-shek

I would like to obtain a cash advance with my credit card – Je voudrais retirer de l'argent avec ma carte de crédit
zhuh voo-dre ruh-tee-ray duh lar-zhoñ a-vek ma kart duh kray-dee

What is your commission? – Vous prenez combien de commission?
voo pruh-nay koñ-byeñ duh ko-mees-yoñ?

Can you contact my bank to arrange for a transfer? – Est-ce que vous pouvez contacter ma banque pour arranger un transfert de fonds?
es-kuh voo poo-vay koñ-tak-tay ma boñk poor a-roñ-zhay uñ troñs-fer duh foñ?

This is the name and address of my bank – Voilà le nom et l'adresse de ma banque
vwah-la luh noñ ay la-dres duh ma boñk

A large French post office can be confusing with a long row of desks, each providing a specific service. The ones you're most likely to need are those for stamps – *timbres au détail* – and parcels – *colis*. If you just want stamps go to a café with a tobacco counter.

How much is a letter – **to Britain?**
C'est combien pour envoyer une en Grande-Bretagne?
lettre
say koñ-byeñ poor oñ-vwah-yay ōōn *oñ groñd bruh-tan-yuh?*
le-truh

– **to the United States?**
aux États-Unis?
ō zay-ta zōō-nee?

Six two-franc stamps, please – Six timbres à deux francs, s'il vous plaît
see tañ-bruh a duh froñ see voo play

Can I have 6 stamps for – **to Britain?**
postcards
Je voudrais six timbres pour à envoyer en Grande-Bretagne
cartes postales
zhuh voo-dre see tañ-bruh poor kart *a oñ-vwah-yay oñ groñd bruh-tan-yuh*
po-stal

– **to the United States?**
à envoyer aux États-Unis
a oñ-vwah-yay ō zay-ta zōō-nee

I want to send this parcel – Je voudrais expédier ce colis
zhuh voo-dre zex-pay-dyay suh ko-lee

I want to send a telegram – Je voudrais envoyer un télégramme
zhuh voo-dre zoñ-vwah-yay uñ tay-lay-gram

A telegram form please – Un formulaire pour un télégramme s'il
vous plaît
uñ for-mōō-ler poor uñ tay-lay-gram see voo
play

When will it arrive? – Quand est-ce qu'il arrivera?
koñ tes-keel a-ree-vuh-ra?

I want to send this by – Je voudrais envoyer cela en recommandé
registered mail *zhuh voo-dre zoñ-vwah-yay suh-la oñ*
ruh-ko-moñ-day

Using the Telephone

The simplest, but most expensive, way to telephone is from your hotel. Otherwise you can go to a post office – tell the clerk the number you want and she will direct you to a box. For local calls you need a counter (*jeton*) and for longer distances coins, and in some cases, as when phoning outside France, she will dial the call herself and charge you afterwards. In some cafés you use *jetons* or coins, in others you pay afterwards. The number of street telephones is growing – the latest type are in stainless steel and glass boxes. When asking for a telephone number you should not give a string of single digits. If you want, say, 765 4321 you ask for seven hundred and sixty five, forty three, twenty one. You'll find numbers set out on page 110 and the telephone alphabet on page 114.

I would like to make a phone call to Britain	– Je voudrais téléphoner en Grande-Bretagne *zhuh voo-dre tay-lay-fō-nay oñ groñd bruh-tan-yuh*
The number I want is . . .	– Je voudrais le numéro . . . *zhuh voo-dre luh noo-may-rō . . .*
I wish to make a reversed charge (collect) call	– Je voudrais téléphoner en P.C.V. *zhuh voo-dre tay-lay-fō-nay oñ pay-say-vay*
I wish to make a person to person call to . . .	– Je désire téléphoner avec préavis à . . . *zhuh day-zeer tay-lay-fō-nay a-vek pray-a-vee a . . .*
Which box do I use?	– C'est quelle cabine? *say kel ka-been?*
May I use the phone please?	– Est-ce que je peux utiliser le téléphone s'il vous plaît? *es-kuh zhuh puh zōō-tee-lee-zay luh tay-lay-fōn see voo play?*
Do I need a token?	– Est-ce qu'il faut un jeton? *es-keel fō tuñ zhuh-toñ?*
Can I have 3 tokens please?	– Trois jetons s'il vous plaît *trwah zhuh-toñ see :oo play*

Can I speak to Mr Thomas? – Est-ce que je peux parler à Monsieur Thomas?
es-kuh zhuh puh par-lay a muh-syuh tō-ma?

I have a crossed line – Il y a déjà quelqu'un sur la ligne
eel ya day-zha kel-kuñ sōor la leen-yuh

We have been cut off – J'ai été coupé
zhay ay-tay koo-pay

You may hear somebody at the other end of the line telling you:

Allô – Hello
a-lō

Je vous passe M. Thomas – I'm putting you through to
zhuh voo pas muhs-yuh tō-ma Mr Thomas

Ne quittez pas – Hold the line
nuh kee-tay pa

J'essaie d'obtenir la – I am trying to connect you
communication
zhe-say dob-tuh-neer la
ko-mōo-nee-kas-yoñ

La ligne est occupée – The line is engaged (busy)
la leen yet o-kōo-pay

Ce numéro est en – This number is out of order
dérangement
suh nōo-may-rō et oñ day-roñzh-moñ

Vous ne pouvez pas obtenir ce – This number cannot be obtained from
numéro du poste que vous this telephone
utilisez
voo nuh poo-vay pa zob-tuh-neer suh
nōo-may-rō dōo post kuh voo
zōo-tee-lee-zay

Je ne peux pas obtenir la – I cannot obtain this number
communication
zhuh nuh puh pa zob-tuh-neer la
ko-mōo-nee-kas-yoñ

Vous avez la communication – Please go ahead
voo za-vay la ko-mōo-nee-kas-yoñ

If a visit to a doctor is necessary, you will have to pay on the spot. Some of the cost of medical treatment is repayable under reciprocal EEC agreements for British and Irish visitors (form E111 should be obtained before departure), but proper accident and medical insurance is still advisable. Ambulances also have to be paid for: there is no central number for you to dial. Remember that normal body temperature on a centigrade thermometer is about 37°, so a reading of 38° means a temperature of 100°.

There has been an accident	Il y a un accident *eel ee a uñ ax-ee-doñ*
Call an ambulance	Appelez une ambulance *ap-lay zōōn oñ-bōō-loñs*
Get a doctor	Allez chercher un docteur *a-lay sher-shay uñ dok-tur*
He is unconscious	Il a perdu connaissance *eel a per-dōō ko-ne-soñs*
She has been seriously injured	Elle est sérieusement blessée *el ay say-ree-yuh-zmoñ ble-say*
He has been badly hurt	Il s'est fait très mal *eel say fe tray mal*
Can I have an appointment with the doctor?	Est-ce que je peux avoir un rendez-vous avec le docteur? *es-kuh zhuh puh za-vwar uñ roñ-day-voo a-vek luh dok-tur?*
I have cut myself	Je me suis coupé *zhuh muh swee koo-pay*
He has burnt himself	Il s'est brûlé *eel say brōō-lay*
She has a temperature	Elle a de la température *el a duh la toñ-pay-ra-tōōr*
I have had a fall	Je suis tombé *zhuh swee toñ-bay*

I have hurt	**– my arm**
Je me suis fait mal	au bras
zhuh muh swee fay mal	*ō brah*
	– my leg
	à la jambe
	a la zhoñb
He has been stung	– Il s'est fait piquer
	eel say fe pee-kay
She has been bitten	– Elle a été mordue
	el a ay-tay mor-dōō
I have broken my arm	– J'ai le bras cassé
	zhay luh brah ka-say
He has dislocated his shoulder	– Il s'est démis l'épaule
	eel say day-mee lay-pōl
She has sprained her ankle	– Elle s'est foulé la cheville
	el say foo-lay la shuh-vee
I have pulled this muscle	– J'ai une élongation de ce muscle
	zhay ōōn ay-loñ-gas-yoñ duh suh mōō-skluh
There is a swelling here	– C'est enflé ici
	set oñ-flay ee-see
It is inflamed here	– C'est enflammé ici
	set oñ-fla-may ee-see
I have a pain here	– J'ai une douleur ici
	zhay ōōn doo-lur ee-see
I find it painful	**– to walk**
Ça me fait mal	de marcher
sa muh fe mal	*duh mar-shay*
	– to swallow
	d'avaler
	da-va-lay
	– to breathe
	de respirer
	duh res-pee-ray

Symptoms

I have	**– a headache**
J'ai mal à	la tête
zhay mal a	*la tet*
	– earache
	l'oreille
	lo-ray
	– a sore throat
	la gorge
	la gorzh
I can't sleep	– Je ne dors pas
	zhuh nuh dor pa
I have sunstroke	– J'ai eu une insolation
	zhay ōō ōōn añ-so-las-yoñ
My tongue is coated	– J'ai la langue pâteuse
	zhay la loñg pah-tuhz
My stomach is upset	– J'ai l'estomac dérangé
	zhay les-to-ma day-roñ-zhay
I feel nauseous	– J'ai envie de vomir
	zhay oñ-vee duh vo-meer
I think I have food poisoning	– Je crois que c'est une intoxication alimentaire
	zhuh krwah kuh set ōōn añ-tox-ee-kas-yoñ a-lee-moñ-ter
I have been sick	– J'ai vomi
	zhay vo-mee
I have diarrhoea	– J'ai la diarrhée
	zhay la dee-a-ray
I am constipated	– Je suis constipé
	zhuh swee koñ-stee-pay
I feel faint	– Je ne me sens pas bien
	zhuh nuh muh soñ pa byeñ

I am allergic –– **to penicillin**
Je suis allergique   à la pénicilline
zhuh swee za-ler-zheek   *a la pay-nee-see-leen*

–– **to cortisone**
à la cortisone
a la kor-tee-zon

I have high blood pressure –– J'ai de la tension
zhay duh la toñ-syoñ

I am a diabetic –– Je suis diabétique
zhuh swee dee-ya-bay-teek

I am taking these drugs –– Je prends ces médicaments
zhuh proñ say may-dee-ka-moñ

Can you give me a French –– Est-ce que vous pouvez me donner des
prescription?   médicaments équivalents?
es-kuh voo poo-vay muh do-nay day
may-dee-ka-moñ zay-kee-va-loñ?

I am pregnant –– Je suis enceinte
zhuh swee zoñ-sañt

I am on the pill –– Je prends la pilule
zhuh proñ la pee-lōōl

My blood group is . . . –– Mon groupe sanguin est . . .
moñ groop soñ-gañ ay . . .

I don't know my blood group –– Je ne connais pas mon groupe sanguin
zhuh nuh ko-ne pa moñ groop soñ-gañ

Must I stay in bed? –– Est-ce que je dois rester au lit?
es-kuh zhuh dwah res-tay ō lee?

Will I be able to go out –– Est-ce que je pourrai sortir demain?
tomorrow?   *es-kuh zhuh poo-ray sor-teer duh-mañ?*

Will I have to go to hospital? –– Est-ce que je dois aller à l'hôpital?
es-kuh zhuh dwah za-lay a lo-pee-tal?

Parts of the Body

Will an operation be necessary?	– Est-ce que je dois me faire opérer? *es-kuh zhuh dwah muh fer o-pay-ray?*
Here is my Elll form	– Voici mon formulaire britannique de sécurité sociale assurance-maladie *vwah-see moñ for-mōō-ler bree-ta-neek duh say-kōō-ree-tay sōs-yal a-sōō-roñs ma-la-dee*
How do I get reimbursed?	– Comment est-ce que je me fais rembourser? *ko-moñ tes-kuh zhuh muh fe roñ-boor-say?*

ankle	la cheville *la shuh-vee*	**kidney**	le rein *luh rañ*
arm	le bras *luh brah*	**knee**	le genou *luh zhuh-noo*
back	le dos *luh dō*	**leg**	la jambe *la zhoñb*
bone	l'os *los*	**liver**	le foie *luh fwah*
breast	le sein *luh sañ*	**lungs**	les poumons *lay poo-moñ*
cheek	la joue *la zhoo*	**mouth**	la bouche *la boosh*
chest	la poitrine *la pwah-treen*	**muscle**	le muscle *luh mōōs-kluh*
ear	l'oreille *lo-ray*	**neck**	le cou *luh koo*
elbow	le coude *luh kood*	**nose**	le nez *luh nay*
eye, eyes	l'œil, les yeux *lye, layz yuh*	**shin**	le tibia *luh tee-bya*
face	le visage *luh vee-zazh*	**skin**	la peau *la pō*
finger	le doigt *luh dwah*	**spine**	la colonne vertébrale *la ko-lon ver-tay-bral*
foot	le pied *luh pyay*	**stomach**	l'estomac *les-to-mah*
hand	la main *la mañ*	**throat**	la gorge *la gorzh*
heart	le cœur *luh kur*	**wrist**	le poignet *luh pwahn-yay*

I need to see the dentist	– Il faut que je voie le dentiste *eel fō kuh zhuh vwah luh doñ-teest*
I have a toothache	– J'ai mal aux dents *zhay mal ō doñ*
It's this one	– C'est celle-ci *say sel-see*
I've broken a tooth	– J'ai une dent de cassée *zhay ōon doñ duh ka-say*
The filling has come out	– Le plombage est parti *luh ploñ-bazh ay par-tee*
Will you have to take it out?	– Est-ce qu'il faudra l'arracher? *es-keel fō-dra la-ra-shay?*
Are you going to fill it?	– Est-ce que vous allez la plomber? *es-kuh voo za-lay la ploñ-bay?*
That hurts	– Ça fait mal *sa fe mal*
Please give me an injection	– Faites-moi une piqûre pour insensibiliser s'il vous plaît *fet mwah ōon pee-kōor poor añ-soñ-see-bee-lee-zay see voo play*
My gums hurt	– Mes gencives sont douloureuses *may zhoñ-seev soñ doo-loo-ruhz*
My false teeth are broken	– Mon dentier est cassé *moñ doñ-tyay ay ka-say*
Can you repair them?	– Est-ce que vous pouvez le réparer? *es-kuh voo poo-vay luh ray-pa-ray?*

The Time

What time is it?	– Quelle heure est-il? *kel ur e-teel?*		
It is . . .	– Il est . . . *eel ay . . .*		
10 o'clock	– dix heures *dee zur*		

5 past 10		cinq	*sañk*
10 past 10		dix	*dees*
a quarter past 10	dix heures	et quart	*ay kar*
20 past 10	*dee zur*	vingt	*vañ*
25 past 10		vingt-cinq	*vañ-sañk*
half past 10		et demie	*ed-mee*

25 to 11		moins vingt-cinq *mwañ vañ-sañk*
20 to 11		moins vingt *mwañ vañ*
a quarter to 11	onze heures *oñ zur*	moins le quart *mwañ luh kar*
10 to 11		moins dix *mwañ dees*
5 to 11		moins cinq *mwañ sañk*

11 o'clock	– onze heures *oñ zur*	
12 o'clock (midday)	– midi *mee-dee*	
(midnight)	– minuit *mee-nwee*	

You may hear the 24-hour clock used when speaking, e.g. –

seize heures vingt *se zur vañ*	1620	4.20 p.m.
dix-neuf heures quarante-cinq *deez-nuh vur ka-roñt-sañk*	1945	7.45 p.m.

The Time

A few of these expressions may be useful.

tonight – ce soir
suh swar

at night – la nuit
la nwee

the morning – le matin
luh ma-tañ

this afternoon – cet après-midi
set a-pre-mee-dee

before midnight – avant minuit
a-voñ mee-nwee

after 3 o'clock – après trois heures
a-pre trwah zur

at half past 6 – à six heures et demie
a see zur ed-mee

nearly 5 o'clock – presque cinq heures
pres-kuh sañk ur

at about 1 o'clock – vers une heure
ver ōōn ur

in an hour's time – dans une heure
doñ zōōn ur

two hours ago – il y a deux heures
eel ee a duh zur

in half an hour – dans une demi-heure
doñ zōōn duh-mee-ur

soon – bientôt
byeñ-tō

early – de bonne heure
duh bon ur

late – tard
tar

Numbers
Up to a million

0	zéro		19	dix-neuf
	zay-rō			*deez-nuhf*
1	un		20	vingt
	uñ			*vañ*
2	deux		21	vingt-et-un
	duh			*vañ-tay-uñ*
3	trois		22	vingt-deux
	trwah			*vañ-duh*
4	quatre		23	vingt-trois
	kat-ruh			*vañ-trwah*
5	cinq		30	trente
	sañk			*troñt*
6	six		40	quarante
	sees			*ka-roñt*
7	sept		50	cinquante
	set			*sañ-koñt*
8	huit		60	soixante
	weet			*swa-soñt*
9	neuf		70	soixante-dix
	nuhf			*swa-soñt-dees*
10	dix		80	quatre-vingts
	dees			*ka-truh-vañ*
11	onze		90	quatre-vingt-dix
	oñz			*ka-truh-vañ-dees*
12	douze		100	cent
	dooz			*soñ*
13	treize		110	cent dix
	trez			*soñ dees*
14	quatorze		200	deux cents
	ka-torz			*duh soñ*
15	quinze		300	trois cents
	kañz			*trwah soñ*
16	seize		1,000	mille
	sez			*meel*
17	dix-sept		2,000	deux mille
	dee-set			*duh meel*
18	dix-huit		1,000,000	un million
	deez-weet			*uñ meel-yoñ*

Numbers
The First to the Last

1st	premier, première	**15th**	quinzième
	pruhm-yay, pruhm-yer		*kañz-yem*
2nd	deuxième	**16th**	seizième
	duhz-yem		*sez-yem*
3rd	troisième	**17th**	dix-septième
	trwahz-yem		*dee-set-yem*
4th	quatrième	**18th**	dix-huitième
	kat-ree-yem		*deez-weet-yem*
5th	cinquième	**19th**	dix-neuvième
	sañk-yem		*deez-nuhv-yem*
6th	sixième	**20th**	vingtième
	seez-yem		*vañt-yem*
7th	septième	**21st**	vingt et unième
	set-yem		*vañ-tay-ōōn-yem*
8th	huitième	**22nd**	vingt-deuxième
	weet-yem		*vañ-duhz-yem*
9th	neuvième	**23rd**	vingt-troisième
	nuhv-yem		*vañ-trwahz-yem*
10th	dixième	**30th**	trentième
	deez-yem		*troñt-yem*
11th	onzième	**40th**	quarantième
	oñz-yem		*ka-roñt-yem*
12th	douzième	**50th**	cinquantième
	dooz-yem		*sañ-koñt-yem*
13th	treizième	**100th**	centième
	trez-yem		*soñt-yem*
14th	quatorzième	**1,000th**	millième
	ka-torz-yem		*meel-yem*

a half	un demi	**a dozen**	une douzaine
	uñ duh-mee		*ōōn doo-zen*
a quarter	un quart	**half a dozen**	une demi-douzaine
	uñ kar		*ōōn duh-mee doo-zen*
a third	un tiers	**the last**	le dernier,
	uñ tyer	**(one)**	la dernière
10%	dix pour cent		*luh dern-yay,*
	dee poor soñ		*la dern-yer*

The Calendar

Sunday	dimanche	**January**	janvier
	dee-moñsh		*zhoñ-vyay*
Monday	lundi	**February**	février
	luñ-dee		*fay-vree-ay*
Tuesday	mardi	**March**	mars
	mar-dee		*mars*
Wednesday	mercredi	**April**	avril
	mer-kruh-dee		*a-vreel*
Thursday	jeudi	**May**	mai
	zhuh-dee		*me*
Friday	vendredi	**June**	juin
	voñ-druh-dee		*zhwañ*
Saturday	samedi	**July**	juillet
	sam-dee		*zhwee-yay*
		August	août
on Friday	vendredi		*oot*
	voñ-druh-dee	**September**	septembre
next Tuesday	mardi prochain		*sep-toñ-bruh*
	mar-dee prosh-añ	**October**	octobre
yesterday	hier		*ok-to-bruh*
	ee-yer	**November**	novembre
today	aujourd'hui		*no-voñ-bruh*
	ō-zhoor-dwee	**December**	décembre
tomorrow	demain		*day-soñ-bruh*
	duh-mañ		
		in June	au mois de juin
spring	le printemps		*ō mwah duh zhwañ*
	luh prañ-toñ	**July 6th**	le six juillet
summer	l'été		*luh see zhwee-yay*
	lay-tay		
autumn	l'automne	**next week**	la semaine
(fall)	*lō-ton*		prochaine
winter	l'hiver		*la smen pro-shen*
	lee-ver	**last month**	le mois dernier
			luh mwah dern-yay
in spring	au printemps		
	ō prañ-toñ		
in summer	en été		
	oñ nay-tay		

Public Holidays

New Year's Day	January 1st
Good Friday	*(Switzerland only)*
Easter Monday	
Labour Day	May 1st *(not Switzerland)*
Ascension Day	
Whit Monday	
National Holiday	July 14th *(France only)*
National Holiday	July 21st *(Belgium only)*
Assumption Day	August 15th *(not Switzerland)*
All Saints' Day	November 1st *(not Switzerland)*
Armistice Day	November 11th *(not Switzerland)*
Christmas Day	December 25th
St Stephen's Day	December 26th *(not France)*

If you are travelling in Switzerland, it is worth remembering that each canton has its own local holidays.

The Alphabet

A	comme	Anatole	N	comme	Nicolas
a	*kom*	*a-na-tol*	*en*	*kom*	*nee-kō-la*
B	for	Berthe	O	for	Oscar
bay		*bert*	*ō*		*os-kar*
C		Célestin	P		Pierre
say		*say-les-tañ*	*pay*		*pyer*
D		Désiré	Q		Quintal
day		*day-zee-ray*	*kōō*		*kañ-tal*
E		Eugène	R		Raoul
uh		*uh-zhen*	*er*		*ra-ool*
F		François	S		Suzanne
ef		*froñ-swah*	*es*		*sōō-zan*
G		Gaston	T		Thérèse
zhay		*gas-toñ*	*tay*		*tay-rez*
H		Henri	U		Ursule
ash		*oñ-ree*	*ōō*		*ōōr-sōōl*
I		Irma	V		Victor
ee		*eer-ma*	*vay*		*veek-tor*
J		Joseph	W		William
zhee		*zhō-zef*	*doo-bluh-vay*		*weel-yam*
K		Kléber	X		Xavier
ka		*klay-ber*	*eex*		*zav-yay*
L		Louis	Y		Yvonne
el		*loo-ee*	*ee grek*		*ee-von*
M		Marcel	Z		Zoé
em		*mar-sel*	*zed*		*zō-ay*

ABBREVIATIONS

AOC	Appellation d'origine contrôlée *(guarantee of the quality of a wine)*
CEE	Communauté économique européenne *(the Common Market)*
M°	Métro
NF	Nouveaux francs *(new francs)*
P & T	Postes et télécommunications *(French Post Office)*
PMU	Pari mutuel urbain *(French Betting Board)*
RATP	Régie autonome des transports parisiens *(Paris Transport Executive)*
SNCF	Société nationale des chemins de fer français *(French Railways)*
TVA	Taxe sur la valeur ajoutée *(Value Added Tax, VAT)*
VDQS	Vin délimité de qualité supérieure *(good quality wine)*

Descriptions

First a list of colours:

beige	beige *bezh*	**mauve**	mauve *mōv*
black	noir *nwar*	**orange**	orange *o-roñzh*
blue	bleu *bluh*	**pink**	rose *rōz*
brown	brun *bruñ*	**purple**	violet *vee-o-le*
cream	crème *krem*	**red**	rouge *roozh*
fawn	fauve *fōv*	**silver**	argenté *ar-zhoñ-tay*
gold	doré *do-ray*	**tan**	ocre *ok-ruh*
green	vert *ver*	**white**	blanc *bloñ*
grey	gris *gree*	**yellow**	jaune *zhōn*

and a few other handy adjectives:

bad	mauvais *mō-ve*	**interesting**	intéressant *añ-tay-re-soñ*
big	grand *groñ*	**little**	petit *puh-tee*
cold	froid *frwah*	**long**	long *loñ*
dark	sombre *soñ-bruh*	**new**	nouveau *noo-vō*
dear	cher *sher*	**old**	vieux *vyuh*
fast	rapide *ra-peed*	**short**	court *koor*
good	bon *boñ*	**slow**	lent *loñ*
hot	chaud *shō*	**terrible**	affreux *a-fruh*

Conversion Tables

lb =	kg		Exchange Rates	
2.2	1	0.45	£1 =	$1 =
4.4	2	0.91	5 francs =	
6.6	3	1.4	10 francs =	
8.8	4	1.8	25 francs =	
11	5	2.2	50 francs =	
13.2	6	2.7	100 francs =	
15.4	7	3.2	150 francs =	
17.6	8	3.6	500 francs =	
19.8	9	4.1	1,000 francs =	
22	10	4.5		
lb =	**kg**			

inches =	cm		feet =	metres	
0.39	1	2.54	3.3	1	0.3
0.79	2	5.08	6.6	2	0.61
1.18	3	7.62	9.9	3	0.91
1.57	4	10.6	13.1	4	1.22
1.97	5	12.7	16.4	5	1.52
2.36	6	15.2	19.7	6	1.83
2.76	7	17.8	23	7	2.13
3.15	8	20.3	26.2	8	2.44
3.54	9	22.9	29.5	9	2.74
3.9	10	25.4	32.9	10	3.05
4.3	11	27.9			
4.7	12	30.1			
inches =	**cm**		**feet** = **metres**		

Conversion Tables

Kilometres	Miles	Centigrade	Fahrenheit
10	6.2	0	32
20	12.4	5	41
30	18.6	10	50
40	24.9	15	59
50	31	17	63
60	37.3	20	68
70	43.5	22	72
80	49.7	24	75
90	56	26	79
100	62	28	82
110	68.3	30	86
120	74.6	35	95
130	81	37	98.4
140	87	38	100
150	93.2	40	104
160	100	50	122
200	124	100	212
300	186		
500	310		

TYRE PRESSURES

lb/sq in	15	18	20	22	24	26	28	30	33	35
kg/sq cm	1.1	1.3	1.4	1.5	1.7	1.8	2	2.1	2.3	2.5

LITRES	UK GALLONS	US GALLONS	LITRES	UK GALLONS	US GALLONS
5	1.1	1.3	25	5.5	6.5
10	2.2	2.6	30	6.6	7.8
15	3.3	3.9	35	7.7	9.1
20	4.4	5.2	40	8.8	10.4

Place Names

Aix-en-Provence	*ex-oñ-pro-voñs*	**Carcassonne**	*kar-ka-son*
Aix-les-Bains	*ex-lay-bañ*	**Carnac**	*kar-nak*
Albi	*al-bee*	**Chamonix**	*sha-mo-nee*
Amiens	*am-yeñ*	**Chantilly**	*shoñ-tee-yee*
Angers	*oñ-zhay*	**Chartres**	*shar-truh*
Angoulême	*oñ-goo-lem*	**Cherbourg**	*sher-boor*
Annecy	*an-see*	**Clermont-Ferrand**	*kler-moñ-fe-roñ*
Antibes	*oñ-teeb*	**Compiègne**	*koñ-pyen-yuh*
Arles	*arl*	**Deauville**	*dō-veel*
Arras	*a-ra*	**Dieppe**	*dee-yep*
Arromanches	*a-ro-moñsh*	**Dijon**	*dee-zhoñ*
Auxerre	*o-ser*	**Dinan**	*dee-noñ*
Avignon	*a-veen-yoñ*	**Dinard**	*dee-nar*
Avranches	*a-vroñsh*	**Dunkerque**	*duñ-kerk*
Bayeux	*bye-yuh*	(Dunkirk)	
Beaune	*bōn*	**Épernay**	*ay-per-nay*
Belle-Île-en-mer	*bel-eel-oñ-mer*	**Évreux**	*ay-vruh*
Benodet	*be-nō-day*	**Foix**	*fwah*
Biarritz	*bee-ya-reets*	**Fontainebleau**	*foñ-ten-blō*
Bordeaux	*bor-dō*	**Fougères**	*foo-zher*
Boulogne	*boo-lon-yuh*	**Fréjus**	*fray-zhōō*
Bourges	*boorzh*	**Genève**	*zhuh-nev*
Brest	*brest*	(Geneva)	
Bruges	*brōōzh*	**Grasse**	*gras*
Bruxelles	*brōō-sel*	**Grenoble**	*gruh-nō-bluh*
(Brussels)		**Hyères**	*yer*
Caen	*koñ*	**Juan-les-Pins**	*zhōō-oñ-lay-pañ*
Calais	*ka-lay*	**la Baule**	*la bōl*
Cannes	*kan*		

Place Names

La Rochelle	*la ro-shel*	**Perpignan**	*per-peen-yoñ*
Lausanne	*lō-zan*	**Poitiers**	*pwaht-yay*
le Havre	*luh av-ruh*	**Pontivy**	*poñ-tee-vee*
le Mans	*luh moñ*	**Quimper**	*kañ-per*
Liège	*lee-ezh*	**Quimperlé**	*kañ-per-lay*
Lille	*leel*	**Reims**	*rañs*
Limoges	*lee-mozh*	**Rennes**	*ren*
Lourdes	*loord*	**Rouen**	*roo-oñ*
Lyon	*lee-yoñ*	**St Brieuc**	*sañ bree-uh*
Marseille	*mar-say*	**St Étienne**	*sañ tay-tyen*
Metz	*mets*	**St Malo**	*sañ ma-lō*
Mont St Michel	*moñ sañ mee-shel*	**St Nazaire**	*sañ na-zer*
Monte Carlo	*moñ-tay-kar-lō*	**St Tropez**	*sañ tro-pay*
Montpellier	*moñ-pel-yay*	**Sète**	*set*
Morlaix	*mor-le*	**Strasbourg**	*straz-boor*
Mulhouse	*mōō-looz*	**Toulon**	*too-loñ*
Nancy	*noñ-see*	**Toulouse**	*too-looz*
Nantes	*noñt*	**Tours**	*toor*
Narbonne	*nar-bon*	**Trébeurden**	*tray-bur-den*
Neuchâtel	*nuh-sha-tel*	**Troyes**	*trwah*
Nevers	*nuh-ver*	**Valence**	*va-loñs*
Nice	*nees*	**Val d'Isère**	*val dee-zer*
Nîmes	*neem*	**Verdun**	*ver-duñ*
Orléans	*or-lay-oñ*	**Versailles**	*ver-sye*
Paris	*pa-ree*	**Vichy**	*vee-shee*
Pau	*pō*	**Vincennes**	*vañ-sen*
Périgueux	*pay-ree-guh*	**Vitre**	*vee-truh*

Accès aux quais –	This way to the trains
Appuyez –	Push
Arrêt –	Stop
Ascenseur –	Lift (elevator)
À vendre –	For sale
Baignade interdite –	No bathing
Caisse *(in shop)* –	Pay here
(in bank) –	Desk
Chaud (C) –	Hot
Complet –	Full
Dames –	Ladies
Défense de fumer –	No smoking
Défense de marcher sur les pelouses –	Keep off the grass
Dégustation –	Sampling *(of wine, oysters etc)*
En panne –	Out of order
Entrée gratuite *or* **libre** –	No obligation to buy
Fermé –	Closed
Froid (F) –	Cold
Fumeurs –	Smokers
Gendarmerie –	Police
Hommes –	Gentlemen
Libre –	Vacant

Signs & Notices

Libre-service –	Self service
Maintenez le loqueteau levé-	Lift the handle – the doors open
l'ouverture des portes	automatically
est automatique	
Messieurs –	Gentlemen
Ne pas toucher –	Do not touch
Non-fumeurs –	Non-smokers
Occupé –	Engaged
Ouvert –	Open
Peinture fraîche –	Wet paint
Poussez –	Push
Prière d'attendre –	Please wait
Service compris –	Service included
Service non compris –	Service not included
Soldes –	Sale
Sonnez –	Ring
Sortie –	Exit
Syndicat d'initiative –	Tourist Information Office
Tirez –	Pull

Index

Index

Index

Personal Details

Name
Nom

Home address
Adresse

Tel

Address in France
Adresse en France

Tel

In case of accident notify
En cas d'accident prévenez

Tel

Passport No.
Passeport No

Car No
No d'immatriculation

Blood group
Groupe sanguin